HOLLYWOOD
Knits

HOLLYWOOD Knits

Thirty Original Suss Designs
SUSS COUSINS

Photographs by Karen Knauer

A LARK PRODUCTION

STEWART, TABORI & CHANG NEW YORK

contents

Thirty Suss Designs

introduction

KNITTING USED TO BE something your mother or grandmother taught you to do. But when our mothers and grandmothers took jobs outside the home and joined aerobics classes and otherwise shifted their attention to matters beyond the domestic arts, knitting came close to falling off the lifestyle radar. Luckily for everyone, knitting has made a thoroughly modern comeback.

The beginnings of the current knitting boom seem to have coincided with the first time Bill Cosby walked onto the set of *The Cosby Show* wearing one of my sweaters. Fueled ever since by the dozens of celebrities who have taken up the craft (and shopped at my store)—Julia Roberts, Sandra Bullock, and Daryl Hannah all knit—and the abundance of hand-knits in top designer collections—Donna Karan, Michael Kors, and Ralph Lauren all feature knits—the knitting resurgence continues to grow, attracting young and old. Women twenty to thirty-five are the fastest-growing segment of the market, with the number of knitters under age thirty-five soaring from 3 percent nationwide in 1998 to 15 percent in 2000, a 400 percent increase. College students knit in droves (there's a famous knitting circle called the Knit-wits at Swarthmore College). And men account for 4 percent of the growing knitting market. I've seen a forty-something male contestant on *Who Wants To Be A Millionaire* tell Regis Philbin that knitting was his favorite way to relieve stress.

More and more people have turned to knitting for the same reasons they take up jogging, gardening, or yoga: it's relaxing and it's therapeutic.

Knitting is also easy to learn. Simple repetition of two basic knitting stitches yields quick and satisfying results. Time spent knitting is not only a way to relax, it is purposeful and produces beautiful handmade gifts and clothing with only a small investment of time. I'd like to let everyone in on this ancient but new-all-over-again craft and the pleasures of creating something out of little more than a few wisps of wool. Knitting is as portable as a book—and I hope my book will make knitting as common a sight as those romance paperbacks!

my knitting life

THE FIRST THING you should know about me, since you're putting yourself in my knitting hands, is that I'm Swedish. I was born and raised in Angelholm, a small Swedish village a few miles northeast of Denmark's Elsinore, where Shakespeare's Hamlet is set. I remember my mother and grandmother during those long, cold winter nights in Sweden knitting by the fire, or making a heavenly meal or a rich dessert in the kitchen. When I was seven, I picked up my first knitting needles. I wanted to make my older brother a sweater, but instead it fit my grandfather, who's always been the lucky one. What I remember most of all is the delicious sense of satisfaction I felt having actually finished my very first project. I've been knitting ever since then, and the time seems right to help make it easy for other people to enjoy that same pleasure.

But the kind of knitting gratification I'm talking about has nothing to do with old-fashioned Fair Isle pullovers or argyle socks. I didn't move to New York, tend bar at night, and knit by day in my East Village studio only to wind up with stuff my grandmother—or yours—could make. I explored art galleries and museums to discover the deep secrets of color: how artists during the Renaissance used gold and embossed copper to make reds and blacks pop, or how some Abstract Expressionists mixed hot pink with orange to make a painting look like it's from another world. I hunted down hole-in-the-wall yarn shops to find unusual wool, and I started mixing yarns to create my own distinctive look: ostrich feathers with a fine silk yarn; furry eyelash with nubby Marokko;

all-white rayon with just a touch of fluffy nylon called Voilà. Once I had a look and feel I liked, I experimented with designs: long coats, fuzzy neck warmers, sexy sweaters. I developed a style using clean simple silhouettes with rich medieval colors and flourishes like crosses and fleurs-de-lis, a look one friend later christened "baroque modern." Eventually, I started selling my creations to acquaintances and friends.

Soon after I arrived in New York, I met and married my husband, who is an actor, so it was natural that other actors began wearing my designs. One of my first customers, Noelle Beck, used to act on the TV soap opera *Loving,* and she became my best friend. After she wore Suss designs on her show, everybody wanted one, including Bill Cosby. I've made more than thirty sweaters for him, probably more than for any one else except my husband. The first time I met Bill, I was brought by limo to his television studio in Astoria, Queens, where I was to measure him. His assistant stood there without a word while I measured Bill's arms again and again, thinking I must be doing something wrong because one was shorter than the other. Finally, the assistant casually mentioned that Bill had been in an accident—had I noticed his arms were different lengths? (If you're ever in New York, you can actually see a Suss Cosby sweater in the American Museum of the Moving Image, where it's on permanent display, thanks to Bill.)

If Bill Cosby was a challenge to fit, imagine what it was like to knit for Magic Johnson! He ordered fourteen sweaters at once, chenille, V necks, lots of stripes. He's as sweet as he is tall—his sweaters were really long. When I hand-delivered them to his home, the main thing I noticed was the hundreds of pairs of sneakers he owned. He had one whole room just for his sneakers.

We moved to Los Angeles in 1991 for my husband's career and to raise our family in a warm, sunny place. Knitting turned out to be the perfect career for a mother. I could knit anytime, when my daughters were napping or playing or at night. At first, I ran my business right out of our home, which made it easy to keep an eye on the children. As they grew, so did my company, and in 1995 I realized it was time for a big beautiful retail shop.

my store

IN ANGELHOLM I HAD OWNED a store called Thanks when I was nineteen, but I decided to open my first American boutique on Beverly Boulevard, L.A.'s fashion row, where my neighbors are designers such as Eduardo Lucero and Richard Tyler. The store is open and airy with warm wood shelves and antique metal accents. I wanted to create a welcoming atmosphere, so I have bowls of glogg—Swedish mulled wine—and anise cookies for customers. It seems to work because the shop is almost like a clubhouse for knitters and knitting students, browsers, and shoppers. My friend Julianne Moore, whom I knew when we both lived in New York, comes in whenever she's in town because she likes to wear my clothes. Of course, she makes them look fabulous. Actresses Jada Pinket Smith and Rhea Perlman come in to buy gifts for their friends and family—and themselves. Kelly Preston buys dresses for her daughter and Elisabeth Shue bought my booties for her baby. Julia Roberts is a great kind of

customer. First, she is a knitter herself and she loves the exotic yarns we sell, and second, she looks great in my knitwear. Both she and Sandra Bullock bought a car coat of mine, Julia in blue and Sandra in black. Sandra's an incredible knitter herself, and she's always coming by the store to pick up baby gifts or a special yarn for her own projects.

Last Christmas Eve, my friend and customer Laurence Fishburne was on his way to Australia to shoot a movie, but he stopped by to introduce his fiancée, Gina Torres, and to show her the store. It turned out that she had been a customer of mine for a long time. They were buying presents, including a *Monsters Inc.* pullover for kids and a hand-crocheted purse for her sister. Together they bought a long, hand-dipped couture coat, which is perfect because *The Matrix,* one of his films that I also designed sweaters for, inspired this piece. Gina bought a dress in the same line.

The people who shop at my store, stars or not, like the look and fit of the sweaters, scarves, coats, dresses, blankets, and bags I design and that my staff hand-knits or makes on a hand loom in the back of the store. My latest line is full of asymmetrical shapes and zippers going vertically, horizontally, or any way I can put them. My silhouettes are clean and mostly fitted or shaped. One dress, for example, has a mix of ten different yarns in vertical and horizontal stripes in the front in gold, silver, red, blue, and mustard tones, with mauve ruffles. It's an insane piece for the insane L.A. lifestyle!

But I also design clothes that are very easy and wearable. Years ago, when we first became friends, Laurence Fishburne bought a simple orange and black chenille sweater that he wore when he appeared on *Sesame Street*. Eventually, he asked me to knit him another one exactly the same: the first one had worn out.

I have racks of needles and baskets of wool on offer as well. You'd be amazed at how many people walk in to buy a baby blanket and walk out with a kit to make the matching hat and booties. Once they see piles of gorgeous yarn in all those delicious colors they can't resist trying to knit something themselves.

about my classes

IT WAS ONLY A MATTER OF TIME before customers asked me to teach knitting, and as I love sharing the joy of creating, I happily accommodated their requests. Knitting is my yoga. It enables me to relax, focus, and be creative. You can use it as a relaxation technique, lowering your shoulders, breathing in on one stitch and out on the next, perhaps lighting a candle or two. I set the stage with the atmosphere in my special knitting room at the store, where I hold classes. There's a beautiful antique metal chandelier above an eight-foot blond wood table, where the beginners sit. I need to be able to walk around and keep them on their toes! My more advanced knitters sit on a honey-colored brocade couch and comfy, red-gold brocade chairs with big pillows. The large, sunny room has light floaty white curtains. It's very soothing—and very baroque modern.

Students come in with great enthusiasm and want to start on huge projects immediately. But if they're beginners, I stop them. My whole approach is knitting fast and

RIGHT: *My Tuesday evening beginner's class enjoying themselves.*

knitting easy. I say, "You're here because you want to learn something very cool and new. I want you to learn a lot right away. I want you to achieve something you feel good about. You can give it to somebody or keep it yourself. It will look great, I promise. So, from the first stitch you learn to make today, try to think about what you want to make."

When they talk about what they want to knit, naturally they wind up talking about their lives. I serve glogg and always lots of food—green apples, fontina cheese, caviar, or little shrimp sandwiches. I want students to let down their hair while they knit, and there's nothing like platters of delicious food to get a bunch of women chatting and munching. Food is a huge topic, of course—our favorite recipes, the latest trendy restaurant.

It's a group of women, after all, getting to know each other, talking about everything at the same time. Someone decides to make a hat for her boyfriend, and soon we hear all about how she's a ski widow. Or one woman's friend is having a baby, and she wants to know how to knit a really easy little cardigan. But then we wind up talking about whose biological clock is ticking—and how men sometimes have a slight problem with commitment. It's like a knitting club—even the experienced knitters want to join the beginners' class it's so much fun.

Model Kirsty Hume has been in my class for a long time. She is very creative and not afraid to take on a project. She started with an easy, comfortable sweater and now she is doing lace knit! When she bought her first house, she said, "I'm walking around with unpacked boxes, but I'm too excited to stop knitting."

The minimum a person needs to know in order to knit something is so little. My class is eight hours, and even halfway through it students know how to cast on, knit, purl, create ribbing, change colors, bind off, decrease, and increase. That's basically all you need to know.

Rose McGowan took my knitting classes for a year, although at first she wasn't sure it would be good for her glamorous image to be pegged as a knitter. These days, of course, it makes her seem all the sexier. Rose chose fast, easy projects. She loved to knit brightly colored stoles and tube tops in fat Marokko yarn with big needles. Now that she has a TV series, *Charmed,* she buys yarn more often than taking a class.

Comedian Julia Sweeney, on the other hand, was determined to use skinny needles on fine cotton for her first project, a sweater. I warned her, "It's going to take you a long, long time." Julia said, "That's okay." She traveled a lot but always came back to the knitting class. The sweater very slowly got bigger and bigger. It took her forever, six months at least.

Usually in the first class I teach how to cast on and how to do the knit stitch. There's a lot of energy, and I walk around and massage students' shoulders a little bit to calm them down. The students walk out of that first class as if they've had something new added to their life.

Although you may not be able to take my classes, I can share with you that knitting *livsglädje*—Swedish for "joie de vivre." Curl up with this book, a glass of wine, some wonderful yarn you can't wait to get your hands on, a pair of the lightest bamboo needles, . . . and knit on!

julia sweeney

I STARTED TAKING KNITTING CLASSES from Suss on Tuesday nights, and I'd never knit before. Suss patiently explained that we should pick an easy project for our first knitting endeavor—a scarf, a hat, or possibly an infant sweater. Full of optimism and blindly in love, I decided to knit my boyfriend a sweater—an extra large man's sweater. My knitting is tight and the yarn I chose was tight. All spring I knit that navy blue sweater with one gray stripe along the bottom. All summer I labored on. Others in the class were on either their fourth or fifth project while I was still working on the sweater. The sweater almost became an additional member of the knitting class, and each week everyone examined my progress—my slow *slow* progress.

I finally finished the sweater in the fall, and the whole class had a celebration. Suss gave me a small square of leather, which I inscribed with my eternal love and stitched it in as a label. Thrilled that it was finished, I put it on and danced around the room. The next day I was leaving for Idaho to meet my boyfriend who was coming back from a hunting trip. He knew about the sweater (How could he not? I was knitting constantly!), but I don't think he ever thought I would actually finish it. Anyway, I flew to Idaho, gave him the sweater, and two days later he broke up with me. (The details of why are too mundane and boringly complicated to retell here.) When I came back to my knitting class, everyone turned to me with expectant faces because the whole class felt they had helped knit that sweater. When I told them that he had ended our relationship, it was as if I had enraged an entire army—of all the people I knew, I swear they were the angriest and most upset about my breakup. I thought they were going to rise up, take off to Idaho, and strangle him with the damn sweater itself.

Anyway, the moral of this story is: 1.) *Never knit a man a sweater unless you have been married to him for over two years.* I think the sweater just becomes this big heap of neediness to some guys, and it is too scary that you would do that much for them—especially when they know deep down they would never take 1000 hours to do something for you. 2.) *Your knitting friends are your friends for life.* Do not underestimate their love and kinship. Also, do not underestimate their wrath. 3.) *Knit for children.* If you don't have any, find some and start knitting for them.

I knit several other things after the sweater fiasco, so this did not end my knitting career—I love it and will continue for my whole life.

ABOVE: *Julia and I share a laugh with her daughter, who is wearing my Big Heart Pullover.*

choosing projects

JUST AS I TELL MY STUDENTS at the first class to go home and think about what they'd most like to make, I suggest you do the same, especially if you're a beginning knitter. Think about what would give you the most pleasure— starting with a gift for someone or creating an indulgent treat for yourself. Maybe you have a special occasion coming up, like a baby shower or bridal shower. Having a gift goal can be great motivation when you're a beginning knitter. On the other hand, if you feel you need to gain some self-confidence, you might be more comfortable picking a project that only you will closely inspect. A colorful scarf is a quick, instant gratification project that fits the bill.

If you've already been knitting for a while, your only decision will be to decide which design to try first. Browse through the thirty projects in the book and notice which pages make you stop and say, "Oooohhhh." Then check the knitting level. I've divided each design into one of three categories:

Cinchy for Starters is easy enough for your first project. It means the item is very fast to knit, uses a simple stitch, and requires no shaping and little finishing.

Step Up and Knit is the next step. These projects might take slightly more time and involve some shaping, sewing, or other finishing, but they are still relatively basic in terms of stitches. Once you've done even one Cinchy for Starters design, go ahead to Step Up and Knit.

Hot Knitters are for readers who've gained a bit more experience. The patterns might take longer, need more attention to shaping and sizing, or have more stitch variation. Or maybe they're for Hot Knitters because the yarn is a little finer and trickier to handle. But even my Hot Knitters projects are not what I'd call difficult or challenging. None of the patterns in this book, for instance, have complicated shaping or require any expert skill.

how to knit a suss design

WHEN YOU KNIT the American or English way, you have to move your whole arm to grab the yarn and wrap it around the needle. Beginning knitters remember how to knit using this sweet rhyme:

In through the front door,
Once around the back,
Peek through the window,
Off jumps Jack!

My technique, the Scandinavian or Continental technique, is called "picking it up." You don't have to let the garment go with one hand and wrap the other around the needle. This makes it easier on your fingers and hands. I wish I could say we had a more sophisticated way to remember what we're doing, but it's another nursery jingle:

Under the fence,
Catch the sheep,
Back we come,
Off we leap!

It seems like nonsense now, but when you follow these directions, you'll understand what this means.

Knitting and purling are quite easy when you knit the Scandinavian way. That's why I can knit and watch a whole movie without looking down. This is incredibly handy since many of my friends—not to mention my husband—are actors, so I spend a lot of time watching movies.

So cue up *Breakfast at Tiffany's* in your VCR or DVD player, follow my easy steps, and you'll be knitting by the time the credits roll. If you've never picked up a pair of needles before, make it easy on yourself: use the largest size you can find and the thickest, smoothest yarn to practice these steps until you feel like a natural.

Scandinavian or Continental Knitting

CASTING ON

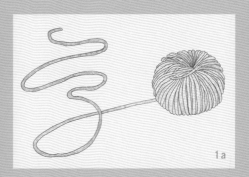

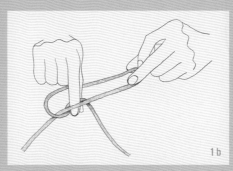

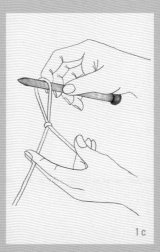

Suss Step 1

Leave a long tail, and make a slip knot and place it on your favorite knitting needle. Twist the yarn, short or tail end over ball end, right over left, forming a loop. Pick up yarn from tail end with index finger and thumb, and pull this strand up through the loop. Insert needle through new loop, and pull to tighten the slip knot. Voilà! This slip knot is your first stitch.

Suss Step 2

Hold the needle with the slip knot in right hand. Wrap the tail or short end of yarn around your left thumb. Drape yarn from ball over your left index finger. Gently pull the two ends of yarn apart to tighten the loop on needle. Keep both strands of yarn resting in the palm of your left hand with your middle, ring, and pinky fingers holding them down.

Suss Step 3

Insert tip of your needle up through loop on thumb, then move needle around strand of yarn on index finger. Bring needle back down through the thumb loop.

Suss Step 4

Drop the thumb loop and pull on short end of yarn with your thumb to make stitch tighten. You now have two stitches on your needle. Repeat Suss Steps 2 through 4 until you have cast on as many stitches on needle as you need according to pattern directions.

2

3a

3b

4

KNIT STITCH

In Europe, we hold the yarn with the left hand and scoop yarn from the left index finger onto the right needle. We control the yarn tension with the last two fingers and the index finger. With practice, knitting this way means you keep your movements to a minimum and therefore increase your speed. If you can hold your needles lightly, it should feel very comfortable to knit the Scandinavian way.

Suss Step 1

Hold needle with cast on stitches in right hand. Wrap the yarn over your left hand as shown.

Suss Step 2

Holding yarn behind work, insert the right needle into the first stitch, from left to right.

Suss Step 3

Angle the tip of the right needle under the yarn to

draw a loop through the stitch. Move the stitch on the left needle toward the top at same time. This should eventually be like one quick movement.

Suss Step 4

Let the stitch slide off the left needle, taking care not to allow any other stitches to slip off. The loop you just made stays on the right needle as the new stitch.

Suss Step 5

Repeat Suss Steps 1 through 4 for each stitch on the left needle, pushing stitches forward on left needle with thumb, index, and middle fingers, moving stitches back on right needle with the thumb.

At the beginning and end of each stitch, the yarn is at the back of the work. All the new stitches will be on the right needle and the left needle will be empty at the end of each row.

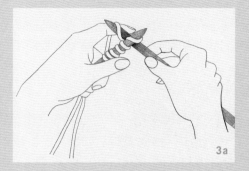

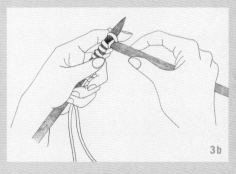

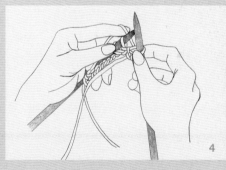

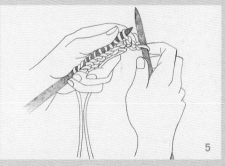

PURL STITCH

Suss Step 1

Insert right needle from right to left through the front loop (nearest you) of the stitch on the left needle. Keep the yarn in your left hand at the front of the needles.

Suss Step 2

Lay the yarn over the right needle from front to back. Be very careful not to lay the yarn from back to front and pick it, which will result in twisted stitches.

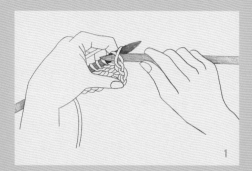

Suss Step 3

Hold the yarn taut, and with the tip of the right needle, pull the yarn through, and keep it on the right needle.

Suss Step 4

Let the stitch slide off the left needle, taking care not to allow any other stitches to slip off. The loop you just made stays on the right needle as the new stitch.

Suss Step 5

Repeat steps one through four for each stitch on the left needle, pushing stitches forward on left needle with thumb, index, and middle fingers, moving stitches back on right needle with the thumb.

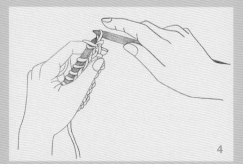

OTHER TIPS AND TECHNIQUES

In addition to the basic knitting stitches, you will need to know how to do the following few things to complete the projects in this book.

Changing Yarn or Carrying It

To switch from one kind or color of yarn to another within a pattern, make a loop with the new yarn around the strand of yarn on the needles. Then start knitting with the new yarn, letting the old yarn drop away.

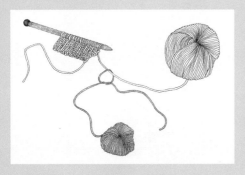

Yarn Over

Make a new stitch and a hole by placing the yarn over the right-hand needle.

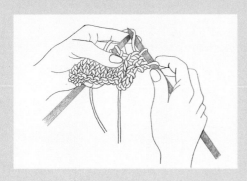

Picking Up Stitches

Insert one needle one full stitch in from the neck edge. Wrap the yarn around the needle, as in knitting. Pull the loop through to form a stitch on the needle. Along a vertical edge of the neck opening you may not need to pick up every stitch, since there are more rows per inch than stitches per inch.

Sewing a Seam with Yarn

Thread a tapestry needle with the same
yarn used for pattern. Holding two sides
of the pattern flat and together, push needle
through tops of each final row. Skip one
stitch, then push the needle back into
skipped stitch. Continue in every stitch
until seamsare closed. Weave in ends.

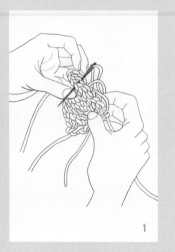

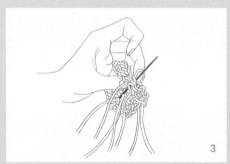

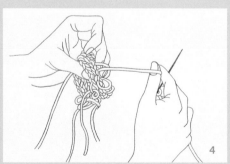

Finishing a Hat

Cut yarn, leaving a 10" tail. Thread tail through the stitches beginning at the opposite end of the piece from the tail. Remove the needle from the stitches and pull tail tightly like a drawstring to close top of hat.

Making Pom-Poms

Cut 40 strands of yarn, each approximately 5" long. Bundle them together and tie tightly around the middle with a long strand of yarn. Trim to even and round pom-pom.

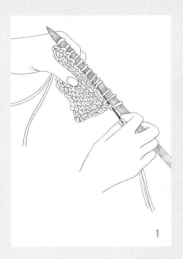

1

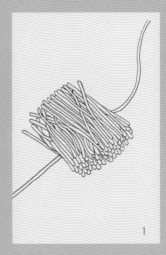

1

2

2

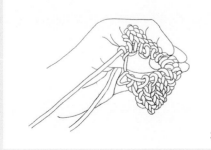

3

3

good yarns

THE YARN IS EVERYTHING when you knit. I like to think of yarn as my raw material the way a fine carpenter works with wood or a painter with her palette. It's my first inspiration in coming up with a new design. I fall in love with a yarn—its color or the way it feels in the skein or how it looks when I try a stitch or two—and then I figure out what I can make out of it. There are endless varieties of yarn, from the finest Italian cotton to the bulkiest sheep's wool. More common are alpaca and llama, angora, cashmere, cotton, linen, ramie, hemp, mohair, silk, wool, rayon, and nylon.

Quality is important when choosing yarn, since better-quality yarns are usually easier to knit with. Beginners should shy away from the cheapest acrylic yarn to avoid frustration. Besides, better yarn doesn't have to mean more money.

two-needle trick

I tell my students to cast on using two needles because otherwise beginners always cast on too tightly. Stick two needles in and pull the yarn until tight on the needles. In your left hand hold the yarn while in your right hold the needles. Then, when you start to knit, pull one needle out, and the stitches move much easier on your needle. (It doesn't matter which needle you pull out when you start knitting.) If you find that this is too tight or if you are using a bulky yarn, you can use just one needle to cast on.

MY FAVORITE YARNS

ONCE I FIND A YARN I LOVE, I tend to design with it over and over again. You can buy any of these yarns at my store or on my website, or through the suppliers I list on pages 121–125.

Marokko

This yarn is thick as rope, so you can whip up almost anything in a matter of minutes. Have an hour? You've got a scarf. Made in Germany, it's single ply instead of twisted so flaws simply don't appear in your knitting. To me it looks like cotton candy.

LaGran Mohair

I've used this mohair ever since I started knitting in Sweden. It comes in bright colors and is soft and lightweight when loosely knit. I made my first baby sweater for my own newborn in black LaGran with tiny gold buttons. When she wore it with little leopard leggings, she was a huge success.

Naturwolle

I first saw a yarn like Naturwolle at a crafts fair in Los Angeles, where a woman was spinning it by hand and selling tiny little skeins for large amounts of money. Then a few weeks later, I found Naturwolle, which was very similar to the hand-spun yarn, at a big yarn fair. Manufactured in Germany, it's hand-spun and hand-dyed Shetland wool and comes in amazing colors: fuchsia, orange, turquoise, red. It's definitely expensive, about $22 for a $3^1/_2$-ounce skein. But I love it because it's bulky, with so much life in it.

The texture is terrific because the yarn itself varies from thick to thin and the color keeps changing as you go along. It's so bumpy that it's great for beginners: mistakes don't show!

Naturwolle begs you to be creative. I can't resist using it for everything from a turtleneck to leg warmers to the cell phone case because it's that versatile. I also love to mix it with a neutral color like ivory for a whole new look: sort of like wearing a lime green bag with your basic black suit. If you're more conservative, Naturwolle comes in blacks and browns, soft baby pastels, and gorgeous muted colors. I have an elegant friend who only wears Gucci and Prada, so she made the cell phone case in the more subdued rust Naturwolle.

Goa

This is a spongelike yarn that floats through your fingers. I highly recommend this yarn for beginners. When the movie *Scooby Doo* was being shot in Australia where it's very hot, we used this yarn for Velma's turtleneck because it's a cool cotton-acrylic but looks thick.

Voilà

Made in Italy, the mecca of fine yarns, this is a very expensive 100 percent polyamide. I use it for the most feminine items because it's one of the softest yarns you can find in the world. My girls can't stop touching it.

Hand-dyed Angora

This yarn is so fine and soft, you almost want to make undergarments with it. I like to use it for baby booties because it's cuddly enough for tiny feet. I discovered it at a yarn fair and got to create my own hues, which made it even more incredible. Although it doesn't take a lot of yarn to make something, it looks substantial in a finished project.

YARN WEIGHTS

THE YARNS I LIST for the designs in this book are my first choices, but I've provided suggestions for substitutions whenever possible. In choosing wool, it helps to know a bit about how yarns are classified, which is mostly by "weight" or thickness as well as fiber content or actual material such as cotton, wool, or rayon.

Here are the most common yarns, from lightest to heaviest:

Fingering (also called Baby)

Gauge of 7 to 8 stitches to the inch on needles from sizes 0 to 3. It can be of any fiber, any number of plies. Use it to knit socks, baby items, shawls, and very lightweight sweaters.

Sport Weight

Gauge of 6 stitches to the inch on sizes 3 to 5 needles.

DK Weight

This is "double knitting" yarn, not Donna Karan. We've always used this weight in Europe, and I notice it's still unfamiliar to American knitters. DK yarns knit at 5 1/2 stitches to the inch on size 6 needles, so it's between sport and worsted.

Worsted

The most familiar weight, gauge is usually 5 stitches to the inch and needle size ranges from sizes 6 to 9. Worsted weight is used to knit nearly every kind of item you can imagine, from baby accessories to afghans.

Chunky

A bit thicker than worsted weight, designed to knit at 4 to 4 1/2 stitches to the inch on sizes 8 to 10 needles.

Bulky

This is my favorite weight of yarn for beginners. With a gauge of 3 1/2 stitches to the inch, it knits up unbelievably quickly. A 40" sweater is only 140 stitches around, which makes for semi-instant gratification.

Superbulky

This weight lets you finish a scarf in an hour. These yarns knit at a gauge of 2 to 2 1/2 stitches to the inch on size 13 or larger needles.

knitting needle abcs

YOU MAY ONLY BE FAMILIAR with those aluminum needles you can pick up in any general store, and that's fine. They're economical, easy to knit with, the weight is nicely balanced, and they're my preferred everyday needles. I like cool metal against my hand. I did all Bill Cosby's sweaters with metal needles. Silver is my favorite, and I happen to love that homey sounding click of metal needles. But bamboo is my second choice because they're

lightweight, very smooth, feel very comfortable in your hand, and come in all sizes. Most importantly, they don't click, which comes in handy when you're knitting while watching TV with your husband and you don't want to annoy him.

Advanced knitters can become obsessed with needles, and that can be fun. Knitting needles come in different lengths and configurations, such as double pointed or circular. I hardly ever find a need for using specialized needles. Honestly, I don't think it matters that much what kind of needles you use. To knit all thirty patterns in this book, you only need four needle sizes, so you don't have to invest a fortune in knitting needles. Comfort and personal aesthetics are all you need to choose among different types. Besides bamboo and aluminum, these include the following:

birch
casein
ebony
nickel-plated
plastic
rosewood
shetland lace
steel
walnut

Some of these needles I never use and don't recommend. Rosewood needles, for example, are too long. But I love the Swallow casein needles because they come in such wild colors—yellow, hot pink, turquoise—and the fact that are made out of milk protein is delicious.

necessary objects

WHAT I LOVE ABOUT KNITTING is that, besides yarn and needles, there isn't much else you absolutely must have to get started . . . or keep going. The few tools that I do recommend are not only helpful, they come in some fantastic, fun shapes and colors. So, the well-accessorized knitting bag can have the following:

Scissors

Small but sharp are best.

Tape measure

Cloth works better than metal for knitting.

Gauge counter

You'll have to find a specialty shop for this but it's great for accuracy.

Crochet hook

Every knitter ends up using crochet once in a while, for finishing pieces. Crochet hooks come in different sizes for yarn according to letters, from A through S. I use aluminum hooks in crazy colors like lime and fuchsia.

Needle point protector

This is like a rubber corkscrew for your knitting needle. Ever since my daughters were little, I've been careful to use needle stoppers to avoid accidents. But they're really for preventing the yarn from slipping off the pointed end of the needle.

Sewing needles

Every girl needs closure! I always indicate using yarn to sew pieces of a knit pattern together, so you need to have a collection of oversized tapestry needles to accommodate its thickness.

I FILL A CUTE BAG made of chiffon with these items to sell in the store as a little kit. You could easily create your own, for yourself or as a great gift.

RIGHT: *From birch to bamboo, knitting needles come in all sorts of sizes and materials. This is my grandmother's collection of needles.*

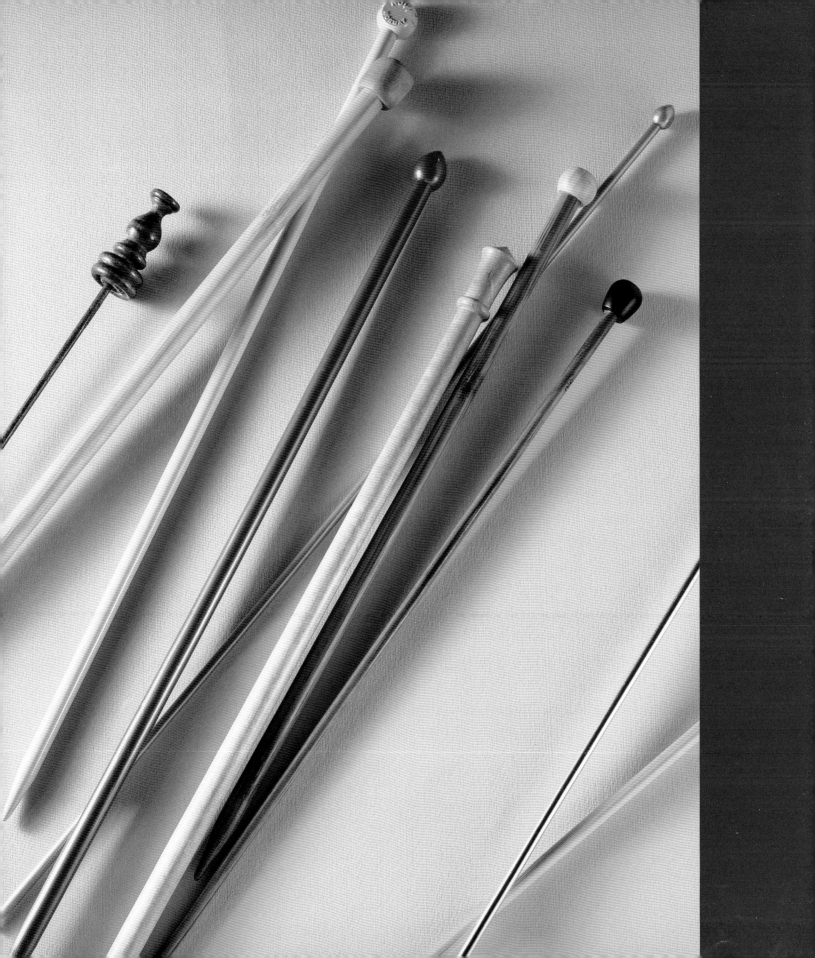

a thousand buttons

ONE OF THOSE DETAILS I love about knitting is picking just the right button for a piece. Buttons are a fun, relatively inexpensive way to customize something. Once you find a button you love for a given item, you have to knit the button holes. It's not hard, as I show you in some of the patterns that use buttons for closure. You measure the buttons to figure out the gauge.

I have a huge collection of buttons. About eighteen years ago I found a family-run Boston fabric store called Saftlers, and they would send me hundreds of buttons at a time: glass buttons, tortoiseshell buttons, silk buttons, marble and metal buttons.

We sell buttons now in my shop. Those made out of wood and shell like abalone are very popular. I found a man who makes coffee cup buttons for me. But when I stumble onto certain really special buttons, I can't bear to sell them. I have carved fish buttons and buttons with a knife, fork, and spoon on the back.

A button can be like a piece of jewelry on a woman's cardigan. Leather buttons are more masculine. I use brushed metal angel buttons on most of my baby things. Sometimes I even make my own buttons out of clay and bake them in the oven. A button can take you places, suggest different moods and styles. If you find a button you love, don't worry about what you'll use it for. Just start collecting and I promise eventually you'll have the perfect piece of knitting to button up.

gauge

BEGINNERS THINK you use one size of needle no matter what you knit. Not so. You can't just pick a pair of needles and expect that what you're knitting is going to come out the same in every yarn. Once you choose the yarn, you always have to knit a swatch, then measure it, and count the stitches up and down. That's called the gauge: the number of stitches and rows per inch you get using any given combination of needles and yarn. No one is gaga over testing gauge—they'd rather be knitting the actual project, not all those little swatches. It's one of those pesky details that really does make a difference in the end result.

It's important to knit enough rows to get an accurate measure of gauge. You want at least 4 inches or more and then measure with either a ruler or a knit gauge tool in the center of your swatch.

What if your sample swatch does not turn out to be the right gauge? If your gauge doesn't come out the same as the gauge called for in the pattern, it could be for a couple of different reasons. It's common to be off 1/4 or 1/2 inch—it depends on your personality and how you knit. Because of your individual energy, maybe you knit too tightly, yet you want yarn to move and be comfortable when you wear it, not constricting.

The yarn itself is alive and can affect the gauge. Darker colors tend to be thicker when you dye them because of the dye process, which absorbs the color. Cream and pastels always come out a little bigger. The variation in yarn is what's great about knitting—it is a handcraft and it looks handmade. Like cooks following a recipe, two knitters can follow a pattern exactly but come out with different results.

But if you're a perfectionist, you should pay extra attention to checking your gauge. Then, if you need to make a correction, simply experiment with your needle size as follows:

If you need fewer stitches to the inch, use a larger needle.
If you need more stitches to the inch, use a smaller needle.

When you hand-knit, close seams with the same yarn. Otherwise you will notice the thread. Sometimes I like to make the finishing show deliberately as an accent. So I'll crochet a sweater together on the outside, as on the baby cardigan on page 62. It gives a little definition and makes a piece special.

the final touches

FINISHING IS NOT ANYBODY'S FAVORITE thing to do, but it is what I like best. It involves sewing, cutting threads, and then steaming to shape the final piece. But when you work on something so long and spend money for that yarn, you should clean it with patience, use the right tools, don't use too small a needle—in other words, when it comes to finishing, it pays to pay attention to detail.

The edges of scarves and blankets can be crocheted for a nice finish. (If you didn't and you were using a stockinette stitch, the sides would roll in instead of lying flat against your body.) To make the sides lie flat, I usually crochet around the edge in a basic whipstitch. It's a masculine stitch, best for men's scarves or boys' baby blankets. I use a shell stitch (see page 74) for hats, pullovers, and girls' things. For a more elaborate finish, I would use a spiderweb stitch, a very romantic soft look. Although they are all easy to do, I've used only the whipstitch and shell stitch in this book.

thirty
suss
designs

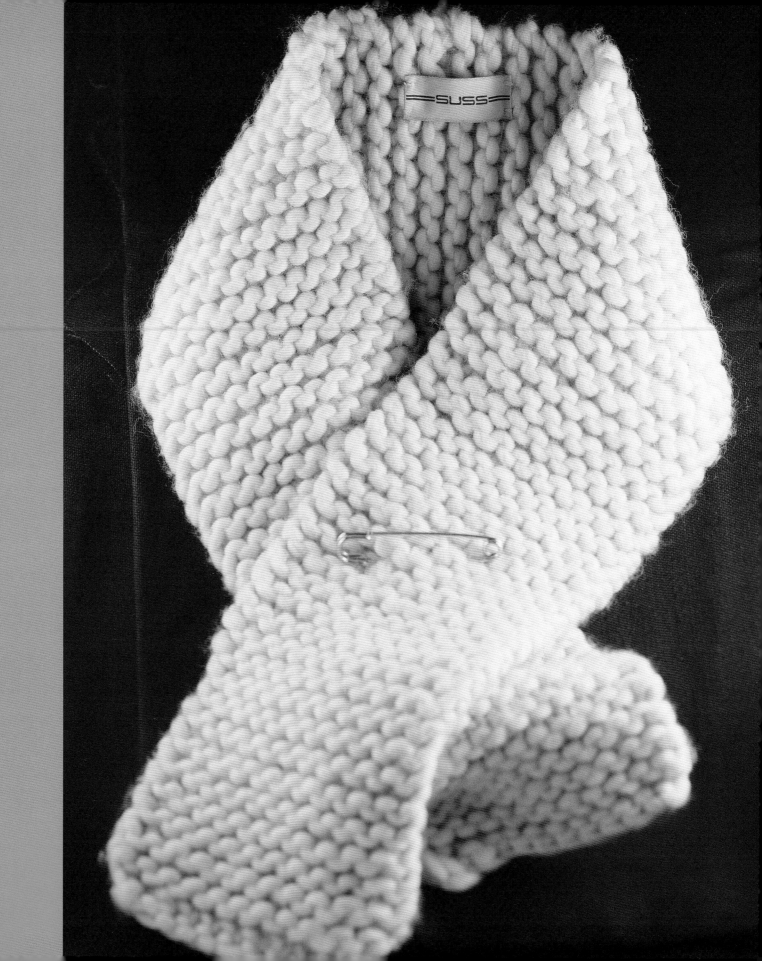

stole scarf
with pin

THIS SJURAL-LOOKING, almost like a piece of art. The pattern is in garter stitch, which is nothing more than knit on both sides. It's fast to knit, and the neutral, in-between color goes with anything. Rose McGowan made the stole because the yarn is her favorite.

You can wear the stole over any top, all year round, and you could wear it over a long, black dress for evening. With a safety pin to close it, what could be simpler? The pin makes it contemporary, although it looks very handmade at the same time. Instead of the safety pin, you might be tempted to use an heirloom broach for elegance, but I think that would make it too little old ladyish. If you knit it wider, it will go down your shoulders more, but then I think you lose the sculptural look.

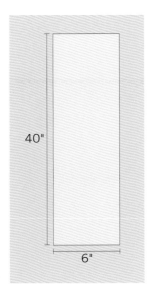

Knitting Level: Cinchy for Starters

Size: One size fits all

Finished Measurements:

Approximately 6" wide and 40" long

Materials:

2 skeins Muench Marokko (100% wool; 88 yards; 200 grams/7 ounces), color #117 cream

1 pair size 15 needles, or size to obtain gauge

Large safety pin, approximately 3" long

Gauge: 2 stitches and 5 rows = 1" in a garter stitch

How to Knit:

Cast on 12 stitches.

Knit every row until piece measures 40" long (approximately 200 rows).

Bind off all stitches.

Finishing:

Weave in ends.

Attach safety pin at center front as desired.

Comparable Yarns:

Any soft, superbulky wool.

LEFT: *You can see my Suss Design label peeking out of this stole.*

nubby scarf
and hat

A WHILE AGO, we had just gotten in a very conservative yarn—khaki with cream spots—and a bright, funky rainbow yarn in the same wool. I was tempted to mix the two. I was flying to New York and brought the yarn with me, not knowing what I'd do with it. But I thought, "I have to make something out of this yarn, I have a good five hours to be productive." As I started knitting and talking to the person next to me, soon others on the plane, including a lot of men, came up and said, "Oh, I used to knit." I was surprised that out of hundreds of people on the plane, I was the only one knitting. I just knitted and knitted and knitted, stepped off the plane, and put on this hat and the scarf. Luckily, that's what I had made because it turned out to be a freezing cold day in New York. I even had had time to tie on the fringe.

The element that gives this version of that original airborne hat and scarf some flair is the addition of rainbow-colored wool with the low-key cream and khaki yarn. The hat is a roll cap that looks good on everyone, men and women. It's basically a rectangle you knit, and then just close the side seams. When you fold it up, you don't see seams. You don't even bind off all the stitches, you just crochet the top, pulling it together, which gives it its rounded shape.

The hat and scarf have a lot of nubby texture and are easy to whip up on big needles. They look like they took much more time and make a perfect gift. No wonder all my students have been making these!

LEFT: *Toss on this hat and scarf and you're wearing a rainbow.*

Knitting Level: Cinchy for Starters

SCARF

Size: One size fits all

Finished Measurements: Approximately $7^{1}/_{2}$" wide and $52^{1}/_{2}$" long, excluding fringe

Materials: 2 skeins Colinette Point Five (100% wool; 55 yards; 100 grams/$3^{1}/_{2}$ ounces), color #134 multicolor

1 skein Muench Naturwolle (100% wool; 110 yards; 100 grams/$3^{1}/_{2}$ ounces), color #193 schaferin

1 pair size 13 needles, or size to obtain gauge

Large crochet hook, any size

Gauge: 2 stitches and $3^{1}/_{2}$ rows = 1" in pattern

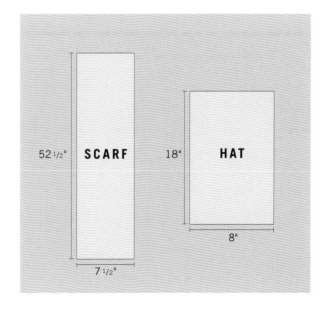

How to Knit:

Cast on 15 stitches with Point Five.

Work pattern as follows:

Rows 1–8: Knit every row.

Row 9: Knit 4, purl 11.

Row 10: Purl 4, knit 11.

Row 11: Knit 4, purl 11.

Rows 12–18: Knit every row.

Row 19: Knit 8, purl 7.

Rows 20–21: Knit every row.

Row 22: Knit 4, purl 11.

Row 23: Purl all stitches.

Row 24: Knit all stitches.

Row 25: Knit 3, purl 12.

Rows 26–28: Knit every row.

Odd Rows 29–39: Knit 5, purl 5, knit 5.

Even Rows 30–40: Purl 5, knit 5, purl 5.

Rows 41–47: Knit every row.

Row 48: Knit 9, purl 2, knit 2, purl 2.

Row 49: Knit 2, purl 2, knit 11.

Row 50: Knit 9, purl 2, knit 2, purl 2.

Row 51: Knit 2, purl 2, knit 11.

Row 52: Knit 3, purl 9, knit 3

Row 53: Knit all stitches.

Row 54: Purl all stitches.

Change to Naturwolle, but do not cut Point Five (See illustration on page 19, Changing Yarn or Carrying It.) Instead, carry the unused yarn along the edge as you work, and proceed as follows:

Rows 55–58: Knit every row.

Rows 59–60: Knit all stitches with Point Five.

Rows 61–64: Knit all stitches with Naturwolle.

Rows 65–66: Knit all stitches with Point Five.

Rows 67–72: Knit all stitches with Naturwolle.

Rows 73–74: Knit all stitches with Point Five.

Rows 75–76: Knit all stitches with Naturwolle.

Rows 77–78: Knit all stitches with Point Five.

Rows 79–84: Knit all stitches with Naturwolle.

Rows 85–86: Knit all stitches with Point Five.

Rows 87–90: Knit all stitches with Naturwolle.

Rows 91–92: Knit all stitches with Point Five.

Rows 93–96: Knit all stitches with Naturwolle.

Rows 97–98: Knit all stitches with Point Five.

Rows 99–102: Knit all stitches with Naturwolle.

Rows 103–104: Knit all stitches with Point Five.

Rows 105–110: Knit all stitches with Naturwolle.

Rows 111–112: Knit all stitches with Point Five.

Rows 113–116: Knit all stitches with Naturwolle.

Rows 117–118: Knit all stitches with Point Five.

Rows 119–122: Knit all stitches with Naturwolle.

Rows 123–124: Knit all stitches with Point Five.

Rows 125–130: Knit all stitches with Naturwolle.

Cut Naturwolle, and using Point Five, only work random pattern in reverse as follows:

Row 131: Purl all stitches.

Row 132: Knit all stitches.

Row 133: Knit 3, purl 9, knit 3.

Row 134: Knit 2, purl 2, knit 11.

Row 135: Knit 9, purl 2, knit 2, purl 2.

Row 136: Knit 2, purl 2, knit 11.

Row 137: Knit 9, purl 3, knit 2, purl 2.

Rows 138–144: Knit every row.

Odd Rows 145–155: Knit 5, purl 5, knit 5.

Even Rows 146–156: Purl 5, knit 5, purl 5.

Rows 157–159: Knit every row.

Row 160: Knit 3, purl 12.

Row 161: Knit all stitches.

Row 162: Purl all stitches.

Row 163: Knit 4, purl 11.

Rows 164–165: Knit every row.

Row 166: Knit 8, purl 7.

Rows 167–173: Knit every row.

Row 174: Knit 4, purl 11.

Row 175: Purl 4, knit 11.

Row 176: Knit 4, purl 11.

Rows 177–184: Knit every row.

Bind off all stitches.

Finishing:

Weave in ends.

To add fringe, cut 12 strands of Point Five and 24 strands of Naturwolle, each 9" long.

Place 6 fringe groups along each short end of the scarf, about 5/8" apart. To make one fringe group, take 1 strand of Point Five and 2 strands of Naturwolle, fold in half. Using crochet hook, pull the loop through edge of scarf, pull tails through loop, and tighten.

HAT

Size: One size fits all

Finished Measurements: 18" around and 7" high

Materials: 1 skein Colinette Point Five (100% wool; 55 yards; 100 grams/3½ ounces), color #134 multicolor

1 skein Muench Naturwolle (100% wool; 110 yards; 100 grams/3½ ounces), color #193 cream

1 pair size 13 needles, or size to obtain gauge

Crochet hook size G

Yarn needle

Gauge: 2 stitches and 3½ rows = 1"

How to Knit:

Cast on 38 stitches with Point Five.

Work in rib pattern as follows:

Row 1: *Knit 2, purl 2; repeat from *to last 2 stitches, end knit 2.

Row 2: *Purl 2, knit 2; repeat from *to last 2 stitches, end purl 2.

Row 3: *Knit 2, purl 2; repeat from *to last 2 stitches, end knit 2.

Row 4: *Purl 2, knit 2; repeat from *to last 2 stitches, end purl 2.

Change to Naturwolle and work in stockinette stitch (alternate rows of knit and purl) as follows:

Row 5: Knit all stitches.

Row 6: Purl all stitches.

Row 7: Knit all stitches.

Row 8: Purl all stitches.

Change to Point Five and work in stockinette stitch as follows:

Row 9: Knit all stitches.

Row 10: Purl all stitches.

Change to Naturwolle and work in stockinette stitch as follows:

Row 11: Knit all stitches.

Row 12: Purl all stitches.

Row 13: Knit all stitches.

Row 14: Purl all stitches.

Change to Point Five and work in stockinette stitch as follows:

Row 15: Knit all stitches.

Row 16: Purl all stitches.

Change to Naturwolle and work in stockinette stitch as follows:

Row 17: Knit all stitches.

Row 18: Purl all stitches.

Row 19: Knit all stitches.

Row 20: Purl all stitches.

Change to Point Five and work in stockinette stitch as follows:

Row 21: Knit all stitches.

Row 22: Purl all stitches.

Change to Naturwolle and work in stockinette stitch as follows:

Row 23: Knit all stitches.

Do not bind off.

Finishing:

Cut yarn, leaving a 10" tail.

Thread tail through the stitches beginning at the opposite end of the piece from the tail. Remove the needle from the stitches, and pull tail tightly like a drawstring to close top of hat.

Sew side seam.

Weave in any remaining ends.

Crochet a chain 4" long with Point Five.

Sew both ends of chain to center top of hat.

Comparable Yarns:

Any bulky, thick-and-thin wool in a solid and a multicolor.

fuzzy
neck warmer

I LOVE TURTLENECKS, but they make me crazy. By the middle of the day, I just want to take them off. So I thought up this "removable" turtleneck. Just as some people like only the tops of muffins, I made just the top of the turtleneck. You can wear a black sweater with one of these neck warmers. Then when you get hot, you can either slip it off or pull it up onto your head as a headband. It's terrific for skiing but also works well in the city. Totally wearable, it makes an unusual but practical gift.

I came up with this yarn combination for the main characters' sweaters in Dr. Seuss's *How the Grinch Stole Christmas* movie. I used a yarn called Eyelash and mixed it with cotton. This yarn is so much fun—it's like wearing a kitty cat around your neck. A soft wool Brown Sheep Company Lamb's Pride may be used instead, especially if the neck warmer is for a man.

Knitting Level: Cinchy for Starters

Size: One size fits all

Finished Measurements: 19" around and 9" tall

Materials:

1 skein Suss Cotton (100% cotton; 174 yards; 113 grams/ 4 ounces), color #2 ivory

2 skeins Trendsetter Eyelash (100% polyester; 77 yards; 20 grams/0.75 ounces), color #223 ivory

1 pair size 10 needles, or size to obtain gauge

Yarn needle

Gauge: 4 stitches and 5 rows = 1" in rib pattern

How to Knit:

Cast on 76 stitches with one strand each of Suss Cotton and Eyelash held together.

Work in rib pattern as follows:

All Rows: *Knit 1, purl 1; repeat from *to end of row.

Repeat this row until piece measures 9" high.

Bind off all stitches.

Finishing:

Sew side seam.

Weave in ends.

Comparable Yarns: Any smooth, worsted weight cotton and any thin, furry yarn.

LEFT: *Film and television actress Regina King is so glamorous in my neck warmer.*

cozy striped
baby blanket with hat

THE PERFECT THING TO WRAP around the stylish baby in a stroller, this blanket is knit in dark raspberry and strawberry ice-cream colors. No one would guess that the content of this merino wool–acrylic baby yarn includes synthetic because its hand is so unbelievably soft. Yet it's not a super-duper fancy yarn. You don't have to spend a fortune to make a baby blanket in any wool because you only need a few small skeins. For a boy or girl baby, the set is a special present. The hat has tassels that match the blanket's tassels.

LEFT: *This baby belongs to a woman in my knitting class. Don't you want to hug her in that hat?*

Knitting Level: Cinchy for Starters

BLANKET

Finished Measurements: 24" wide and 33" long

Materials:

4 skeins Muench Aspen (50% extra fine merino wool, 50% microfiber; 63 yards; 50 grams/1$\frac{3}{4}$ ounces), color #14 light pink

3 skeins Muench Aspen (50% extra fine merino wool, 50% microfiber; 63 yards; 50 grams/1$\frac{3}{4}$ ounces), color #15 rose

1 pair size 11 needles, or size to obtain gauge

Crochet hook size H

Gauge:

2$\frac{1}{2}$ stitches and 4$\frac{1}{2}$ rows = 1" in stockinette stitch

How to Knit:

Cast on 57 stitches with rose Aspen.

Work in stockinette stitch as follows:

Row 1: Knit all stitches.

Row 2: Purl all stitches.

Row 3: Knit all stitches.

Row 4: Purl all stitches.

Row 5: Knit all stitches.

Row 6: Purl all stitches.

Change to pink Aspen and work in stockinette stitch as follows:

Row 7: Knit all stitches.

Row 8: Purl all stitches.

Row 9: Knit all stitches.

Row 10: Purl all stitches.

Row 11: Knit all stitches.

Row 12: Purl all stitches.

Repeat these 12 rows (6 rows rose, 6 rows pink) for stripe pattern 12 times in all until you have 144 rows measuring approximately 32" high.

Bind off all stitches loosely.

Finishing:

Work 1 row of single crochet around all 4 sides of the blanket using pink Aspen.

Weave in ends.

Tassels: Cut 40 strands of pink Aspen, each approximately 15" long. Divide into 4 groups of 10 strands each. Fold 1 group in half, and use crochet hook to pull through corner of blanket to form a loop. Pull ends through loop and tighten. Repeat at remaining 3 corners.

HAT

Size: 3-6 months

Finished Measurements: 14$^{1/2}$" around and 6" high

Materials:

1 skein Muench Aspen (50% extra fine merino wool, 50% microfiber; 63 yards; 50 grams/1$^{3/4}$ ounces), color #14 light pink

1 skein Muench Aspen (50% extra fine merino wool, 50% microfiber; 63 yards; 50 grams/1$^{3/4}$ ounces), color #15 rose

1 pair size 11 needles, or size to obtain gauge

Crochet hook size H

Yarn needle

Gauge: 2$^{1/2}$ stitches and 4$^{1/2}$ rows = 1" in stockinette stitch

How to Knit:

Cast on 36 stitches with rose Aspen.

Work in stockinette stitch as follows:

Row 1: Knit all stitches.

Row 2: Purl all stitches.

Row 3: Knit all stitches.

Row 4: Purl all stitches.

Row 5: Knit all stitches.

Row 6: Purl all stitches.

Change to pink Aspen and work in stockinette stitch as follows:

Row 7: Knit all stitches.

Row 8: Purl all stitches.

Row 9: Knit all stitches.

Row 10: Purl all stitches.

Row 11: Knit all stitches.

Row 12: Purl all stitches.

Repeat these 12 rows (6 rows rose, 6 rows pink) for stripe pattern 3 times in all until you have 36 rows.

Work 6 more rows with rose Aspen as follows:

Row 37: Knit all stitches.

Row 38: Purl all stitches.

Row 39: Knit all stitches.

Row 40: Purl all stitches.

Row 41: Knit all stitches.

Row 42: Purl all stitches.

Do not bind off.

Finishing:

Cut yarn, leaving a 10" tail.

Thread tail through the stitches beginning at the opposite end of the piece from the tail. Remove the needle from the stitches, and pull tail tightly like a drawstring to close top of hat.

Sew side seam with pink Aspen.

Work 1 round of single crochet around bottom edge of hat in pink Aspen.

Weave in ends.

Tassel: Cut 8 strands of pink Aspen, each approximately 8" long. Fold in half, and wrap tightly just below the fold. Sew to top of hat.

Comparable Yarns:

Any soft, washable bulky wool or blend.

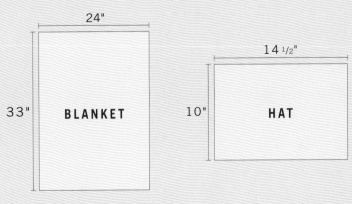

24"

BLANKET

33"

14 1/2"

HAT

10"

bridal
evening bag

I MADE TEN OF THESE BAGS in luscious cream with embroidered gold flowers and lined them with silk douppioni for my friend to give her bridesmaids at her wedding in Sweden. So elegant! To match the bag I gave her crocheted chokers, simple straps that tied around the neck.

The creamy golden color is just right because it goes with practically any wedding party color scheme. It makes a beautiful surprise bridal shower gift. Everyone else usually gives lingerie, so this bag really stands out with its fine stitch and knitted strap. You can put lipstick in it and use it as a traditional evening bag, but a bride could also store it as a keepsake, with wedding day memorabilia tucked inside.

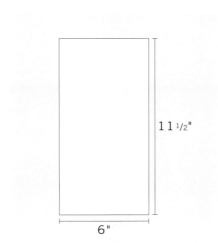

Knitting Level: Cinchy for Starters

Finished Measurements: 6" wide and 5" high

Materials: 1 skein Muench Touch Me (72% rayon, 28% wool; 60 yards; 50 grams/1^{3}/$_{4}$ ounces), color #3624 cream

1 pair size 7 needles, or size to obtain gauge

Crochet hook size H

3 small ivory satin roses (from arts-and-crafts or sewing store)

Yarn needle

Matching sewing thread and needle

Gauge: 4 stitches and 5 rows = 1" in stockinette stitch

How to Knit: Cast on 26 stitches.

Work in stockinette stitch as follows:

Row 1: Knit all stitches.

Row 2: Purl all stitches.

Repeat these 2 rows until piece measures 11^{1}/$_{2}$", or approximately 58 rows.

Bind off all stitches.

Finishing: Fold bag 5" up from beginning of piece with fold positioned at bottom of bag.

Sew side seams.

Work 1 row of single crochet around flap and bag opening.

Weave in ends.

Crochet a chain approximately 25" long, and attach with yarn to upper corners of bag.

Sew on flowers with matching thread, positioned as shown in photograph.

Comparable Yarns: Any bulky chenille.

LEFT: *An elegant gift for any bride or bridesmaid.*

soft-as-a-bunny
makeup case

THE INSPIRATION for this case was the fact that every day I put nearly everything I own in my bag—camera, sunglasses, cell phone, datebook. My bag is always black, so it's like a black hole. I could never find my makeup. With this case, when I'm looking for my lipstick quickly, I put my hand in and feel it right away. The yarn is from Italy, 100 percent nylon but feels like angora from a bunny rabbit. People see it and want to pet it. It's really cute.

The case is pretty stretchy, but if you don't put a lot in it, it doesn't get too heavy. It's not for travel, just for keeping your lipstick and blush in your purse. Actually, when I go out in the evening, I tuck some money in and carry only it.

The tiny tassel gives it a bit of extra flair, and there's a zipper closure. You could line it and work in many other yarns—or knit it in black for a more sophisticated look.

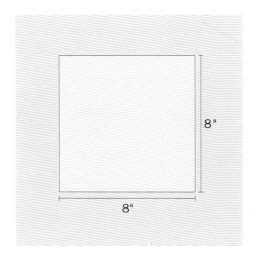

Knitting Level: Cinchy for Starters

Finished Measurements: 8" wide and 4" high

Materials: 1 skein Trendsetter Voila (100% rayon; 180 yards; 50 grams/1¾ ounces), color #10 fuchsia

1 pair size 7 needles, or size to obtain gauge

1 matching zipper 7" long

Matching sewing thread and needle

Gauge: 23 stitches = 4", or 5¾ stitches = 1", in stockinette stitch using double strand of yarn

How to Knit: Wind skein into 2 equal balls of yarn. Holding 2 strands together, cast on 46 stitches. — *I recommend 40 stitches*

Work in stockinette stitch as follows:

Row 1: Knit all stitches.

Row 2: Purl all stitches.

Repeat these 2 rows for pattern until piece measures 8" high.

Bind off all stitches.

Finishing: Fold piece in half with fold positioned at bottom of bag.

Sew zipper to top of bag using matching thread.

Sew side seams.

Weave in ends.

Tassel: Cut 5 strands of yarn, each approximately 12" long. Fold lengths in half and push folded end through zipper pull to form a loop. Pull ends through loop and tighten.

Comparable Yarns: Any nylon fur yarn.

RIGHT: *Makeup case or evening bag—it's your choice.*

superskinny
woolly scarf

IMAGINE A COMBINATION of Halloween and the Fourth of July and you've got a Swedish holiday called Pask. The Thursday before Easter young girls paint their faces, put on long skirts and scarves, and roam from house to house collecting sweet goodies. Meanwhile, the grownups are lighting bonfires to scare off evil spirits, and blasts of fireworks help the girls pretend they're shooting witches out of the sky. I like to think life is just one long Pask celebration, and in that spirit, I designed this wild and woolly scarf for your own private Pask.

The unisex scarf is not only superskinny, it's also superfast to make. You only cast on eight stitches—I first made it on a plane in an hour using a leftover ball of yarn from another project. It's ideal for using yarn you don't know what else to do with. You can wrap it around your neck six times because it's really long. More of an accessory than the other scarves in the book, it goes well with denim jackets and T-shirts.

Knitting Level: Cinchy for Starters

Size: One size fits all

Finished Measurements: Approximately 2" wide and 72" long, excluding fringe

Materials:

1 skein Muench Naturwolle (100% wool; 110 yards; 100 grams/3½ ounces), color #80 Pastell

1 pair size 15 needles, or size to obtain gauge

Crochet hook size G

Gauge: 4 stitches and 2½ rows = 1" in rib pattern

How to Knit: Cut 20 strands of yarn each 20" long. Set aside to attach later as fringe.

Cast on 8 stitches.

Work in rib pattern as follows:

All Rows: Knit 2, purl 2, knit 2, purl 2.

Repeat this row until you have reached the desired length or until you run out of yarn.

Bind off all stitches.

Finishing: Weave in ends.

Place 5 evenly spaced fringe groups along each short end of the scarf. To make one fringe group, take 2 strands of precut yarn, fold in half. Using crochet hook, pull the loop through edge of scarf, pull tails through loop, and tighten.

Comparable Yarns: Any soft, bulky wool, preferably a multicolor single ply.

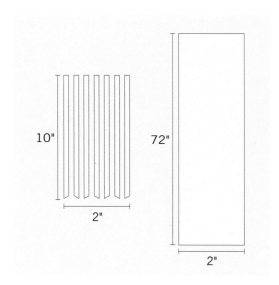

RIGHT: My older daughter, Hanna, in my favorite scarf.

ribbed tube
top with tie

THIS VERSATILE TOP LOOKS GREAT in chunky Aspen yarn, which is incredibly soft. It's more sophisticated than a straight tube top because of the rib. Wear it three ways: tied around your neck or the straps criss-crossed in either back or front. With two buttons on each side, you can adjust the straps to fit and look just right. You can wear it any time of year: alone in warm weather or under a jacket when it's cooler. For a longer look, just add a few inches at the bottom. It's so easy to make, too—you knit two straight pieces, sew the side seams together, and you're set to go.

LEFT: *Tube top modeled by Youki Kudoh, a high profile actress and writer in Japan. Youki has done several American films, including* Snow Falling on Cedars.

Knitting Level: Cinchy for Starters

Sizes: Small (medium, large)

Finished Measurements: 29" (30$\frac{1}{2}$", 32") around

Materials:

3 (3, 4) skeins Muench Aspen (50% extra fine merino wool, 50% microfiber; 63 yards; 50 grams/1$\frac{3}{4}$ ounces), color #13 black

1 pair size 10$\frac{1}{2}$ needles, or size to obtain gauge

4 buttons, $\frac{3}{4}$" each

Yarn needle

Gauge: 2$\frac{1}{2}$ stitches and 4$\frac{3}{4}$ rows = 1" in rib pattern

How to Knit: Cast on 36 (38, 40) stitches.

Work in rib pattern as follows:

Row 1: *Knit 2, purl 2; rep from * to last 0 (2, 0) stitches, end knit 0 (2, 0).

Row 2: Purl 0 (2, 0) stitches, *knit 2, purl 2; repeat from * to end.

Repeat these 2 rows of rib pattern until piece measures 13 (14, 14$\frac{1}{2}$)" from beginning, approximately 62 (66, 68) rows.

Bind off all stitches in pattern.

Make a second piece the same as the first.

Finishing: Sew 2 pieces together at sides.

Cut 12 strands of yarn approximately 108" long. Working with 3 groups of 4 strands each, make a 36" long braid. Secure the ends of the braid.

Weave in ends.

Sew a pair of buttons to inside of back, placing them 5½"
from side seam and 1" and 2" down from the top edge. Sew
the remaining pair of buttons 5½" from the other side seam,
1" and 2" down from the top as before. There is no need for
buttonholes in the strap as the braid provides natural holes.

Comparable Yarns:

Any soft bulky yarn that matches the gauge.

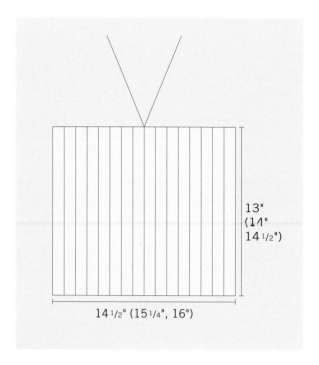

13"
(14"
14½")

14½" (15¼", 16")

chunky tote

THIS IS A TOTE FOR EVERYTHING! It knits up fast in sturdy hot pink Marokko wool, so it's a very popular project in my knitting classes. You use the same yarn for the handles but knit it on smaller needles. A huge wooden button closure in dark and light rosewood is gorgeous. For a more elegant touch, use a shell button. Abalone makes it look like it's perfect for a walk on the beach.

You might think about lining the tote, depending on what sort of stuff you'll be tossing into it. If so, just cut a piece of fabric and stitch it in.

Knitting Level: Step Up and Knit

Finished Measurements: Approximately 12" wide, 8¹/₂" high, and 4" deep

Materials:

3 skeins Muench Marokko (100% wool; 88 yards; 200 grams/7 ounces), color #63 fuchsia

1 pair size 13 needles, or size to obtain gauge

1 pair size 15 needles, or size to obtain gauge

Crochet hook size I

1 wooden button, 1¹/₂"

Yarn needle

Gauge:

2 stitches and 5 rows = 1" in garter stitch using larger needles

How to Knit:

BODY

Using larger needles, cast on 24 stitches.

Work in garter stitch (knit all stitches every row) until piece measures 21" long, approximately 105 rows.

Bind off all stitches.

SIDES

Using larger needles, cast on 8 stitches.

Work in garter stitch until piece measures 8¹/₂" long, approximately 42 rows.

Bind off all stitches.

Make another side the same as the first.

STRAPS

Using smaller needles, cast on 3 stitches.

Work in garter stitch until piece measures 27" or desired length.

Bind off all stitches.

Make another strap the same as the first.

CLOSURE

Using smaller needles, cast on 3 stitches.

Work in garter stitch until piece measures 7".

Bind off 2 stitches, leaving last stitch open.

Beginning with the last knitted stitch, crochet a chain approximately 4" long.

Attach end of chain to bound-off stitches to form a button loop.

Finishing: Fold body in half with fold positioned at bottom of bag.

Insert side pieces, and crochet sides and body together from the outside.

Sew straps to inside upper edges of body, positioning the end of each strap 1 1/2" from side seams as shown in photograph.

Sew nonloop side of closure to outside of bag, centered between ends of strap.

Weave in ends.

Sew button to upper edge of opposite side of body.

Comparable Yarns:

Any super bulky wool or wool blend in a solid color.

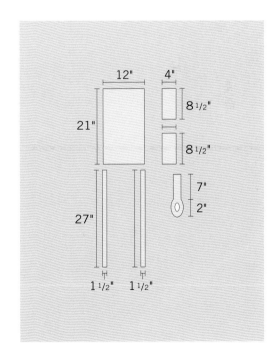

LEFT: *The small tight stitch on the straps prevents the tote from stretching out.*

water
bottle holder

I TRY TO DRINK at least one bottle of water every day, and for a long time my water bottles were always rolling around in my car. (The 16-ounce size doesn't fit in my coffee-cup holder.) So I knit this clever portable water-bottle holder with a strap to hang on the garment hook inside the car. It holds my favorite middle-size bottle. Instead of knitting a solid bottom, I designed a crosspiece that holds the bottom of the bottle like a holster—makes it easier for the knitter. Because it is for water, I, of course, used two different blue yarns.

Knitting Level: Step Up and Knit

Finished Measurements: 10" around and 7" tall, excluding strap

Materials: 1 skein Muench Lame #3 (62% rayon, 38% polyester; 165 yards; 25 grams/0.88 ounces), color #46 silver

1 skein Muench Goa (50% cotton, 50% acrylic; 65 yards; 50 grams/1¾ ounces), color #8 dark blue

1 skein Muench Goa (50% cotton, 50% acrylic; 65 yards; 50 grams/1¾ ounces), color #28 light blue

1 pair size 6 needles, or size to obtain gauge

1 pair size 8 needles, or size to obtain gauge

Yarn needle

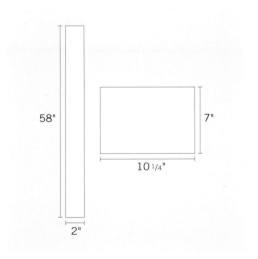

58"

2"

7"

10 1/4"

Gauge:

3½ stitches and 5½ rows = 1", in stockinette stitch using Goa and Lame #3 together on larger needles; 7 stitches and 6 rows = 1" in rib pattern using Goa on smaller needles.

How to Knit:

BODY

Cast on 36 stitches using larger needles and one strand each of Lame #3 and light blue Goa held together.

Work in stockinette stitch as follows:

Row 1: Knit all stitches.

Row 2: Purl all stitches.

Repeat these 2 rows until piece measures 7", approximately 38 rows.

Bind off all stitches.

STRAP

Cast on 15 stitches using smaller needles and a single strand of dark blue Goa.

Work in rib pattern as follows:

Row 1: *Knit 1, purl 1; repeat from * to last stitch, end knit 1.

Row 2: *Purl 1, knit 2; repeat from * to last stitch, end purl 1.

Repeat these 2 rows until strap measures 58".

Bind off all stitches.

Finishing:

Sew body together at one side to form a 7" tall tube.

Sew beginning and end of strap together to form a loop.

Positioning strap seam at the bottom, sew one side edge of strap around body as shown in photograph.

Fold strap in half and sew other side around body, covering the body side seam and leaving remaining portion of strap free.

Weave in ends.

Comparable Yarns:

Any thin metallic yarn and any bulky cotton.

knit
knitting bag

WITH BEAUTIFUL, smooth birch knitting needles built right in as handles, this knitting bag is convenient and brilliant! Just be sure to sew the seam tight enough to keep the needles from falling out. Of course, you don't have to use the bag only for knitting. Some chic women I know carry it as a regular purse. You could even knit the bag combining two yarns such as an Eyelash and a cotton to get an incredible look.

A variation on this pattern is to use all your gauge swatches and make a patchwork bag out of them. Whenever you knit a swatch, you'll need to make it the same size, either a 3" or 4" square. It's also a terrific way to use up left-over balls of yarn. I always hate to throw them out, so I knit odds and ends into squares and sew them together to make a knitting bag.

Knitting Level: Step Up and Knit

Finished Measurements: Approximately 11" wide, 11" high, and 3 1/2" deep

Materials:

1 skein Brown Sheep Company Lamb's Pride Bulky (85% wool, 15% mohair; 125 yards; 114 grams/4 ounces), color #M-05 onyx

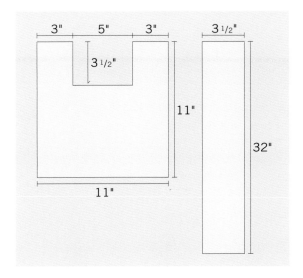

LEFT: *You could make this bag in bright colors for a more summery look.*

1 skein Brown Sheep Company Lamb's Pride Bulky (85% wool, 15% mohair; 125 yards; 114 grams/4 ounces), color #M-130 silver

1 pair size 10 1/2 needles, or size to obtain gauge

1 pair size 17 birch needles for handles (14" length)

"Brittany" yarn needle

Gauge: 2 3/4 stitches and 5 rows = 1" in stockinette stitch

How to Knit:

BODY

With onyx, cast on 32 stitches.

Work in stockinette stitch as follows:

Row 1: Knit all stitches.

Row 2: Purl all stitches.

Repeat these 2 rows 6 more times-14 rows total.

Change to silver, and work in stockinette stitch for 14 rows.

Change back to onyx, and work in stockinette stitch for 13 rows, ending with a purl row.

On the next row, knit 9 stitches, bind off 14 stitches, knit 9 stitches.

Change to silver. Using 2 balls of yarn and working each 9-stitch section separately, work 12 rows stockinette stitch on each section.

Bind off all stitches.

Make a second piece the same as the first.

GUSSET

With onyx, cast on 12 stitches.

Work in stockinette stitch for 32", approximately 160 rows.

Bind off all stitches.

Finishing: Sew gusset to sides and bottom of body, leaving silver sections unattached as shown in photograph.

Fold each silver flap to fit snugly around a size 17 birch needle, and sew securely.

Weave in ends.

Insert size 17 needles as handles.

Comparable Yarns: Any smooth bulky yarn.

cell phone
case

ADMIT IT. Don't you toss your cell phone around with abandon? Haven't you found it on the floor of your car or at the bottom of your pocketbook? When I realized that I was spending almost as much time searching for my cell phone as I was actually using it, I decided it was time to create a solution to my problem.

I worked up this design during some downtime at our booth at a trade show. I was knitting—of course—and trying to perfect that little window the numbers would show through. Passersby soon figured out what I was up to, and the immediate clamoring for this handy cell phone cover was all the proof I needed that I wasn't the only one out there trying to find my cell phone!

This is as soft and safe a nest for a cell phone as anyone could want—and much easier to spot or even feel for among the lipstick, daybook, and other items in your bag. The pattern calls for brightly colored wool yarn, but it would also be striking in cotton mixed with Voila—still as colorful as can be.

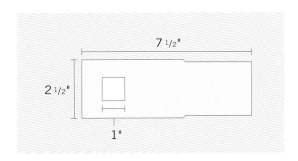

Knitting Level: Step Up and Knit

Finished Measurements: 7" high and 2½" wide, closed

Materials: 1 skein Muench Naturwolle (100% wool; 110 yards; 100 grams/3½ ounces), color #73 Magma

1 pair size 10½ needles, or size to obtain gauge

LEFT: One of my all-time favorite inspirations is this cell phone cover.

2 stitch holders

1 large snap

Crochet hook size I

Yarn needle

Matching sewing thread and needle for attaching snap

Gauge: 3 stitches and 4 rows = 1" in stockinette stitch

How to Knit: Cast on 7 stitches.

Work in stockinette stitch as follows:

Row 1: Knit all stitches.

Row 2: Purl all stitches.

Repeat these 2 rows a total of 15 times, ending with Row 30.

Row 31: Increase 1 stitch at each end—9 stitches.

Continue in stockinette stitch for 34 more rows—65 rows total.

Row 66: Purl 3 stitches and place the stitches just worked on a stitch holder, bind off the center 3 stitches, purl the remaining 3 stitches.

Work 4 rows stockinette stitch on the remaining 3 stitches, then place these stitches on a holder. Cut yarn.

Place the 3 stitches from the first holder on a needle with the knit side facing you, and join yarn, ready to work a knit row.

Work 4 rows stockinette stitch on these 3 stitches.

On the next row, rejoin all stitches as follows: Knit 3, cast on 3 stitches over the gap, knit 3 stitches from second holder—9 stitches.

Work 4 more rows stockinette stitch.

Bind off all stitches.

Finishing:

Fold window section up to just below the point where you increased from 7 to 9 stitches.

Sew side seams.

Work 1 row of single crochet around the flap and top opening.

Weave in ends.

Sew snap to flap bottom of case as shown.

Comparable Yarns: Any soft, bulky wool in multicolor.

sweet baby
cardigan and hat

THIS LOVELY BABY set is hand-crocheted together instead of sewn, and all the stitching is exposed on the outside. Two little pom-poms on the corners of the hat make baby look especially adorable.

This piece calls for a simple, loosely knit yarn, an incredible cotton that has a spongelike feel. You can also make it in a cotton chenille with a crochet whipstitch.

LEFT: *The pom-poms on the hat are easy to make.*

Knitting Level: Step Up and Knit

CARDIGAN

Size: 0–3 months

Finished Measurements: 18" around with 7" sleeves

Materials:

4 skeins Muench Goa (50% cotton, 50% acrylic; 65 yards; 50 grams/1¾ ounces), color #18 cream

1 skein Muench Samoa (50% cotton, 50% acrylic; 104 yards; 50 grams/1¾ ounces), color #52 baby pink

1 pair size 10 needles, or size to obtain gauge

Crochet hook size H

Gauge: 13 stitches = 4", or 3¼ stitches and 6 rows = 1" in garter stitch

How to Knit:

BACK

Cast on 29 stitches with Goa.

Work in garter stitch (knit all stitches every row) until piece measures 9½".

Bind off all stitches.

FRONTS

Cast on 15 stitches with Goa.

Work in garter stitch until piece measures 9½".

Bind off all stitches.

Make a second front the same as the first.

SLEEVES

Cast on 19 stitches.

Work in garter stitch until piece measures 7".

Bind off all stitches.

Make a second sleeve the same as the first.

Finishing:

Using Samoa, single crochet pieces together as given below.

Fold each sleeve in half lengthwise, crochet sleeve seam, then crochet around sleeve cuff.

Crochet fronts to back at shoulder, working the first shoulder seam halfway across the first front piece; then crochet across the back neck opening; and then work the second shoulder seam beginning at the halfway point of the second front piece.

Crochet sleeves to body, matching the midpoint of each sleeve top to the shoulder seam, and stretching each sleeve slightly to ensure correct placement.

Crochet side seams.

Crochet around all remaining edges.

Weave in ends.

For ties, crochet 2 chains, each approximately 10" long, and attach to fronts 3" down from neck edge. If desired, make 2 pom-poms as given in hat finishing instructions below and attach to the end of each chain.

HAT

Size: 0-3 months

Finished Measurements:

12" around with 6¹/2" tall

Materials:

2 skeins Muench Goa (50% cotton, 50% acrylic; 65 yards; 50 grams/1³/4 ounces), color #18 cream

1 skein Muench Samoa (50% cotton, 50% acrylic; 104 yards; 50 grams/1³/4 ounces), color #52 baby pink

1 pair size 10 needles, or size to obtain gauge

Crochet hook size H

Gauge:

13 stitches = 4", or 3¼ stitches and 6 rows = 1" in garter stitch

How to Knit:

Cast on 19 stitches with Goa.

Work in garter stitch (knit all stitches every row) until piece measures 7¹/2".

Bind off all stitches loosely.

Make a second piece the same as the first.

Finishing:

Using Samoa, single-crochet pieces together around 3 sides, leaving 1 short side open, then single-crochet around opening.

Weave in ends.

Fold up bottom edge about 1".

Make 2 pom-poms as follows:

Cut several strands of Samoa, each approximately 2" long.

Bundle them together, and tie tightly around the middle with a long strand of Samoa, and use the ends of the long strand to attach to the top corners of hat.

Comparable Yarns: For Goa, any bulky cotton or cotton blend; for Samoa, any worsted weight cotton or cotton blend.

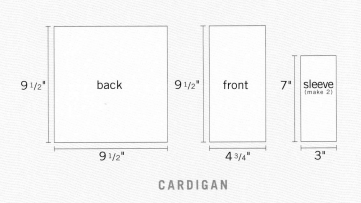

9 1/2" back 9 1/2" front 7" sleeve (make 2)

9 1/2" 4 3/4" 3"

CARDIGAN

7 1/2" 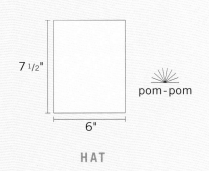 pom-pom

6"

HAT

ballerina
wrap

IN THE OLD DAYS, women in Sweden made wraps like this to keep their shoulders warm when they were knitting. I first saw a picture in an old crochet book, and I turned it into a version for today's woman, who can wear it on top of everything, no matter what she's up to. (Even the very modern Anthropologie catalog carried the wrap my company makes.) You can wear it around your waist, crisscrossed over your chest, around the arms and tied in back, or as a top or stole.

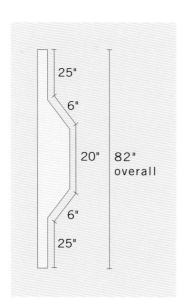

LEFT: *The ballerina wrap is worn crisscrossed but there are at least three other ways to wear it. Be creative!*

Knitting level: Step Up and Knit

Size: One size fits all

Finished Measurements: 82" long and 9" wide

Materials: 2 skeins Classic Elite Yarns LaGran (76.5% mohair, 17.5% wool, 6% nylon; 90 yards; 42.5 grams/1 1/2 ounces), color #6513 black

1 pair size 10 1/2 needles, or size to obtain gauge

Gauge: 3 stitches and 6 1/2 rows = 1" in stockinette stitch

How to Knit: Cast on 7 stitches.

Work in stockinette stitch as follows:

Row 1: Knit all stitches.

Row 2: Purl all stitches.

Repeat these 2 rows for 162 rows, ending with a purl row on Row 162. Piece will measure approximately 25".

Beginning on Row 163, increase 1 stitch at the beginning of every knit row 29 times, ending with a purl row—36 stitches.

Work even (with no further shaping) in stockinette stitch for 130 rows, ending with a purl row.

Piece will measure approximately 20" from the last increase row.

Beginning on the next knit row, decrease 1 stitch at the beginning of every knit row 29 times—7 stitches.

Work even in stockinette stitch for 162 rows, or approximately 25" from the last decrease row.

Bind off all stitches.

Finishing: Weave in ends.

Comparable Yarns: Any worsted weight mohair.

golf club
covers

I FIRST MADE THESE for a TV commercial in which sports broadcaster and football star Howie Long is carrying golf clubs. I knitted footballs on the golf club covers and used black and silver yarn to represent his old team, the Oakland Raiders.

Now we carry them in the store in bright-colored wools for Father's Day and Christmas. I wrap six in a box. They make a perfect gift for those impossible people who already have everything. My girlfriend bought them for her dad, and I embroidered his name on them. You can also embroider the numbers to indicate each golf club. And, of course, plenty of women I know play golf, so don't forget to make some for your gal pals, too.

This pattern is for one golf club cover, but I'm sure you'll want to knit enough for a whole set.

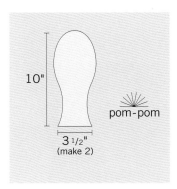

Knitting Level: Step Up and Knit

Finished Measurements: Approximately 7" around and 10" tall, excluding pom-pom

LEFT: *Try personalizing the golf club covers with embroidered monograms.*

Materials:

1 skein Brown Sheep Company Lamb's Pride Bulky (85% wool, 15% mohair; 125 yards; 114 grams/4 ounces), color #M-130 silver

1 skein Brown Sheep Company Lamb's Pride Bulky (85% wool, 15% mohair; 125 yards; 114 grams/4 ounces), color #M-82 blue flannel

1 pair size 9 needles, or size to obtain gauge

Yarn needle

Gauge: 3 3/4 stitches and 5 rows = 1" in stockinette stitch

How to Knit: With blue flannel, cast on 16 stitches.

Work in stockinette stitch as follows:

Row 1: Knit all stitches.

Row 2: Purl all stitches.

Repeat these 2 rows for stockinette stitch, working 6 rows of blue flannel, then 6 rows of silver for stripe pattern.

Work in stripe pattern for 12 rows.

Continuing stripe pattern as established, shape as follows: decrease 1 stitch at each side every 3 rows 4 times—8 stitches.

Work 6 rows even in stripe pattern (without shaping).

Continuing stripe pattern, increase 1 stitch at each side every 3 rows 2 times—12 stitches.

Work even in stripe pattern until piece measures 7½", approximately 38 rows.

Continuing stripe pattern, decrease 1 stitch at each edge every other row 6 times—no stitches remain.

Make a second piece the same as the first.

Finishing: Sew pieces together, leaving an opening at the bottom.

Weave in ends.

Pom-pom: Cut 40 strands of yarn, each approximately 5" long. Bundle them together, tie tightly around the middle with a long strand of yarn, and use the ends of the long strand to attach to the top of golf club cover.

Comparable Yarns: Any bulky cotton or Suss Cotton.

fingerless
gloves

THESE ARE VINTAGE COOL in an elegant camel with cream. I converted this pattern into knitting from an old Swedish crochet book. It was common in nineteenth-century Sweden to wear this kind of glove when you worked outside gathering firewood or tending animals. Today, I'm more likely to spot them on women working the trendiest spots in town.

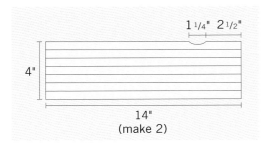

Knitting Level: Step Up and Knit

Size: One size fits all

Finished Measurements: 8" around and 14" long

Materials:

1 skein Classic Elite Yarns Lush (50% angora, 50% wool; 123 yards; 50 grams/1¾ ounces), color #4416 cream

1 skein Classic Elite Yarns Lush (50% angora, 50% wool; 123 yards; 50 grams/1¾ ounces), color #4438 brown

LEFT: *Fingerless gloves are both fashionable and practical in soft camel and cream.*

1 pair size 7 needles, or size to obtain gauge

Yarn needle

Gauge: 5½ stitches and 7 rows = 1" in knit 6, purl 6 rib pattern

How to Knit: With cream, cast on 24 stitches.

Work in knit 1, purl 1 rib pattern for 3 rows as follows:

All Rows: *Knit 1, purl 1; repeat from * to end.

Change to knit 6, purl 6 rib pattern and work as follows:

All Rows: *Knit 6, purl 6; repeat from * to end.

Work in knit 6, purl 6 rib until piece measures 7" from beginning, approximately 50 rows.

Change to brown and continue in rib pattern until piece measures 14" from beginning, approximately 100 rows total.

Bind off all stitches in pattern.

Make 3 more pieces the same as the first.

Finishing: Sew 2 pieces together at one long side, reversing the seam allowance 3½" from the brown end so right side of seam will show when cuff is folded back.

For the other side seam, beginning at the cream end, sew seam for 2½", leave 1¼" open for thumb, and finish seam, reversing seam allowance in the bottom 3½" as before.

At the cream end, create 4 finger holes by sewing ½" seams between the knit and purl stitches.

Weave in ends.

Fold up cuff.

Complete second glove same as the first.

Comparable Yarns: Any soft worsted weight yarn in cashmere, merino, or angora.

luxurious
throw

ONE NIGHT I WAS THROWING a small birthday dinner party for a friend, who was bringing along another couple I didn't know. As I went to the kitchen to get the wife a glass of wine I suddenly realized why she looked so familiar: it was actress Angela Bassett and her husband, actor Courtney Vance. Luckily I had made my special Scampi Indienne, and they were very gracious. Now she shops in the store all the time, and she bought this throw.

I made this blanket in two pieces, splitting it in the center so it wouldn't stretch. I knitted it very tight—it will last forever—and hand-crocheted the two pieces together.

I chose to knit it in white with white cotton crochet stitch. Voila is not a natural fiber, but it feels so real you think you're throwing a fur on your lap. You can use it when you're watching TV or even on a bed. It's very elegant, fancier than a garden-variety afghan because of the yarn and because it's white.

Knitting Level: Step Up and Knit

Finished Measurements:

56" wide and 60" long

Materials:

14 skeins Suss Cotton (100% cotton; 174 yards; 113 grams/ 4 ounces), color #1 white

14 skeins Trendsetter Voila (100% nylon; 180 yards; 50 grams/1 3/4 ounces), color #223 ivory

1 pair size 10 needles, or size to obtain gauge

Large crochet hook, any size

Yarn needle

Gauge: 4 stitches and 5 rows = 1" in stockinette stitch

How to Knit:

Cast on 112 stitches with one strand each of Suss Cotton and Voila held together.

Work in stockinette stitch as follows:

Row 1: Knit all stitches.

Row 2: Purl all stitches.

Repeat these 2 rows until piece measures 60".

Bind off all stitches loosely.

Make a second piece the same as the first.

LEFT: *Stage and television actor Steven Weber and his wife, Juliette Hohnen, curled up under a gorgeous white throw with their one-year-old son, Jack.*

Finishing:

Crochet two halves of throw together using Suss Cotton.

Starting at one corner and using Suss Cotton, work 1 row of shell-trim crochet around all 4 sides of throw as follows:

Chain 2 stitches, work 2 double crochet in same space, skip 3 stitches, work 1 single crochet in following space. Repeat from beginning.

Weave in ends.

Tassels: Cut 100 strands each of Suss Cotton and Voila, each approximately 20" long. Divide into 4 groups of 25 strands each. Fold 1 group in half, and use crochet hook to pull through corner of throw to form a loop. Pull ends through loop and tighten. Repeat at remaining 3 corners.

Comparable Yarns:

Any smooth, worsted weight cotton and any thin furry yarn.

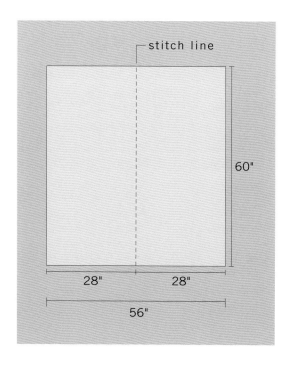

striped patch
pillow with tassels

THIS DESIGN WAS INSPIRED by my grandmother, who liked to use patchwork in lots of different crafts projects, from quilts to potholders to pillows. I remember watching TV with her in the family room, lounging on my favorite red and blue patchwork pillow. Now I like to make my pillows in different tones of the same color.

Knitting Level: Step Up and Knit

Finished Measurements: 15" square

Materials: 2 skeins Classic Elite Yarns LaGran (76.5% mohair, 17.5% wool, 6% nylon; 90 yards; 42.5 grams/1$\frac{1}{2}$ ounces), color #6555 red

2 skeins Classic Elite Yarns LaGran (76.5% mohair, 17.5% wool, 6% nylon; 90 yards; 42.5 grams/1$\frac{1}{2}$ ounces), color #6541 hot pink

1 pair size 10$\frac{1}{2}$ needles, or size to obtain gauge

3 snaps size $\frac{1}{2}$"

Crochet hook size I

Pillow form 15" square

Yarn needle

Gauge: 3$\frac{3}{4}$ stitches and 4$\frac{1}{2}$ rows = 1" in stockinette stitch

How to Knit:

FRONT SQUARES

With red, cast on 30 stitches.

Work in stockinette stitch as follows:

Row 1: Knit all stitches.

Row 2: Purl all stitches.

Repeat these 2 rows for stockinette stitch, working 6 rows of red, then 6 rows of hot pink for stripe pattern.

Work in stripe pattern for 36 rows. Piece will measure approximately 8" high.

Bind off all stitches.

Make 3 more pieces the same as the first.

BACK UNDERFLAP

With hot pink, cast on 57 stitches.

Work in stockinette stitch until piece measures 11",
approximately 55 rows.

Bind off all stitches.

BACK OVERFLAP

With red, cast on 57 stitches.

Work in knit 3, purl 3 rib pattern as follows:

Row 1: *Knit 3, purl 3; repeat from *to last 3 stitches,
end knit 3.

Row 2: *Purl 3, knit 3; repeat from *to last 3 stitches,
end purl 3.

Repeat these 2 rows until piece measures 3½",
approximately 16 rows.

Change to stockinette stitch, and work until piece measures
12½" from beginning.

Bind off all stitches.

Finishing: Sew small squares together to form a large
square with stripes running at right angles as shown in photograph.

Sew hot pink underflap to large front square along 3 sides.

Sew stockinette stitch end of red overflap to open side of front.

Sew sides of red flap to pillow, overlapping the hot pink back.

Weave in any remaining ends.

Sew snaps evenly spaced to underside of ribbed section of red
flap, approximately 1" from the bound off edge.

Sew other half of snaps to corresponding points on hot pink
underflap.

Tassels: Cut 40 strands each of both red and hot pink approximately 18" long. Divide into 4 groups of 10 strands of each
color. Fold 1 group in half and use the crochet hook to pull
through corner of pillow to form a loop. Pull ends through loop
and tighten. Repeat at remaining 3 corners.

Insert pillow form and close snaps.

Comparable Yarns: Any bulky cotton or Suss Cotton.

LEFT: *A couch can never have too
many patchwork pillows. Red and pink
give it even more punch.*

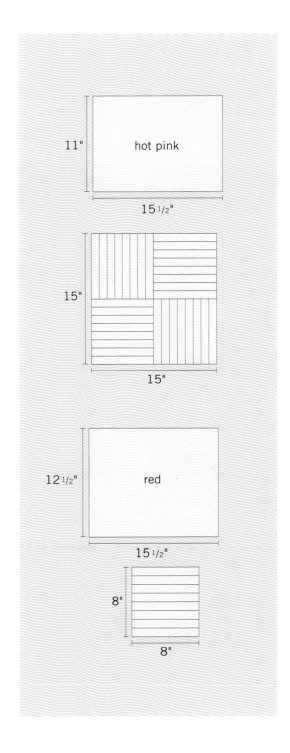

funky ski
hat

YOU JUST HAVE TO SMILE when you see this goofy, funny, character hat, which I first made for Dr. Seuss's *How the Grinch Stole Christmas.* Superlong, it goes all the way down your back. I designed it for people who really want to make a statement—one Hollywood producer bought it in different shades of greens. The hat looks cool on the ski slopes, where everyone seems to dress in funny clothing and original hats are the rage.

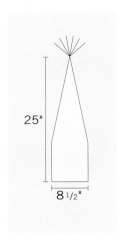

25"

8 1/2"

Knitting Level: Step Up and Knit

Size: One size fits all

Finished Measurements: 17" around and 25" long, excluding tassel

Materials:

2 skeins Classic Elite Yarns LaGran (76.5% mohair, 17.5% wool, 6% nylon; 90 yards; 42.5 grams/1 1/2 ounces), color #6535 light green

1 skein Classic Elite Yarns LaGran (76.5% mohair, 17.5% wool, 6% nylon; 90 yards; 42.5 grams/1 1/2 ounces), color #6503 dark green

1 pair size 9 needles, or size to obtain gauge

LEFT: *Be prepared for smiles whenever you wear this goofy green hat.*

Large crochet hook, any size

Yarn needle

Gauge: 4 stitches and 5 rows = 1" in stockinette stitch

How to Knit:

With light green, cast on 44 stitches.

Work in knit 1, purl 1 rib as follows:

All Rows: *Knit 1, purl 1; repeat from * to end.

Repeat this row until piece measures 5 1/2".

Change to dark green and work stockinette stitch as follows:

Row 1: Knit all stitches.

Row 2: Purl all stitches.

Repeat these 2 rows for stockinette stitch according to the stripe pattern and shaping given below:

Stripe pattern: 20 rows dark green, 20 rows light green, 20 rows dark green, 16 rows light green, 16 rows dark green, 16 rows light green, 8 rows dark green.

Shaping: Work 20 rows even (without shaping), then decrease 1 stitch at each side every 8 rows 6 times, then every 4 rows 8 times, then every other row 7 times—2 stitches remain.

Work on remaining stitches to end of stripe pattern, then bind off all stitches.

Make a second piece the same as the first.

Finishing:

Sew 2 pieces together leaving ribbed end open and reversing the seam allowance halfway up the ribbing so right side of seam will show when ribbed brim is folded back.

Weave in ends.

Tassel: Cut 50 strands of light green, each approximately 18" long. Fold group in half and use crochet hook to pull through tip of hat to form a loop. Pull ends through loop and tighten.

Comparable Yarns:

Any space-dyed, worsted weight wool. Muench Trikolore (100% wool; 77 yards; 100 grams/3 1/2 ounces) makes the hat totally different and even funkier.

angel angora
booties

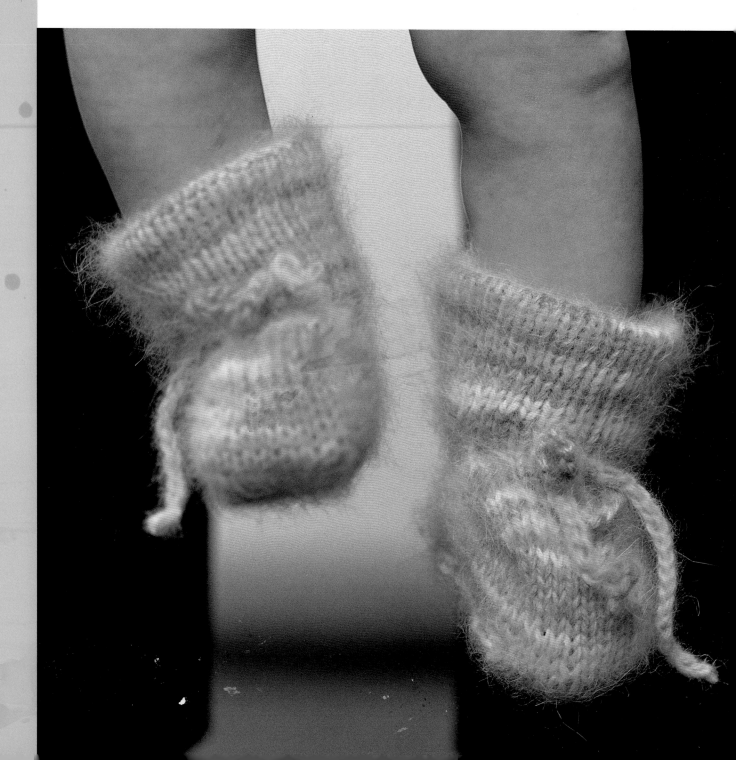

THESE MAKE IDEAL baby shower gifts because the colors are unisex. All the pregnant women in my classes are making these booties now. They have tiny ties so the baby can't kick them off (you wouldn't want to lose these little beauties). The booties use a supersmall yarn and require supersmall needles, but it's a supersmall project, so it doesn't take too long. The yarn is so soft and fluffy that baby looks like a little bunny. I get this angora from a woman who hand-dyes it in her home.

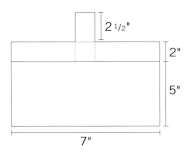

Knitting Level: Hot Knitters

Size: 3-6 months

Finished Measurements:

3¼" long, 3½" high, and 1½" wide

Materials: 2 skeins Lorna's Laces Angel Hand-Dyed Angora (70% angora, 30% wool; 50 yards; 15 grams/0.5 ounces), color #24 Happy Valley

1 pair size 7 needles, or size to obtain gauge

Crochet hook size H

Yarn needle

Gauge: 19 stitches = 4", or 4¾ stitches and 6 rows = 1", in stockinette stitch

LEFT: *These cute baby booties are named after the luxurious yarn I used initially, though any yarn of the same gauge works.*

How to Knit: Cast on 36 stitches.

Work in stockinette stitch as follows:

Row 1: Knit all stitches.

Row 2: Purl all stitches.

Repeat these 2 rows for 28 rows total, ending with a purl row.

Bind off 13 stitches at the beginning of the next 2 rows—10 stitches.

Work even (with no shaping) for 13 more rows, ending with a knit row. Do not turn the work.

With knit side of work facing you, pick up and knit 9 stitches along the side of the flap you just worked, then pick up and knit 13 stitches along the bound off edge—32 stitches.

Purl back across all 32 stitches, then break yarn.

With the other needle and the knit side of work facing you, join yarn at beginning of first bound-off row, pick up and knit 13 stitches along bound-off edge, then 9 stitches along other side of flap.

With the same needle, continue knitting across all stitches from the other needle—54 stitches.

Work 13 rows stockinette stitch on all stitches, ending with a purl row.

Bind off 22 stitches at the beginning of the next 2 rows—10 stitches.

Work even on these 10 stitches for 22 rows, ending with a purl row.

Bind off all stitches.

Finishing: Fold top flap down to line formed by picked-up stitches, and sew around for hem.

Sew back seam.

Sew sole to sides and back.

Weave in any remaining ends.

Braid or make a crochet chain approximately 20" long.

Thread chain through every other stitch around bootie, just under sewn hem. Tie in a bow in front.

Finish second bootie same as the first.

Comparable Yarns: Any yarn that matches the gauge will work for this pattern.

straight neck
pullover

THIS LONG SLEEVE SWEATER has a straight, narrow body with beautiful, long skinny sleeves. It's very Scandinavian in the cut with a flattering boat neckline. I made it in a beautiful sky blue cotton. Using two strands of yarn at the same time gives the fabric a nice hand on big needles. The pullover looks very handmade, almost grandma-knit, yet quite hip.

The neck is easy to make—no shaping at all. For the cap sleeves you do not just bind off the stitches but decrease them gradually. This technique is not difficult, so don't be put off. This is a great fun challenge.

For a slightly less casual look you could also make this in wool. Model Kirsty Hume made it in turquoise wool to hang out in on the weekends. She picked this basic yet sophisticated shape as her first project, one she could really get a lot of use from.

LEFT: *Model Kirsty Hume chose the pullover in blue—great with her coloring, although I like it in a vibrant red too.*

Knitting Level: Hot Knitters

Sizes: Small (medium, large)

Finished Measurements: 32" (34", 36") around

Materials:

5 (5, 5) skeins Suss Cotton (100% cotton; 174 yards; 113 grams/4 ounces), color #10 sky blue

1 pair size 13 needles, or size to obtain gauge

1 stitch holder

Yarn needle

Gauge: 7 stitches = 3", or $2^{1}/_{3}$ stitches and $3^{1}/_{2}$ rows = 1", in stockinette stitch using double strand of yarn

How to Knit:

BACK AND FRONT

Cast on 38 (40, 42) stitches with two strands of yarn held together.

Work in stockinette stitch as follows:

Row 1: Knit all stitches.

Row 2: Purl all stitches.

Repeat these 2 rows for stockinette stitch until piece measures $11^{1}/_{2}$" (12", $12^{1}/_{2}$"), ending with a purl row.

Shape armhole as follows: Bind off 2 stitches at the beginning of the next 2 rows, then decrease 1 stitch at each side of the next knit row—32 (34, 36) stitches.

Work even (with no further shaping) until piece measures 18" (19", $19^{1}/_{2}$") from beginning, ending with a purl row.

Shape shoulders and neck as follows:

Bind off 2 (3, 3) stitches at the beginning of the next 2 rows—28 (28, 30) stitches.

At the beginning of the next knit row, bind off 2 (2, 3) stitches, knit 4 (there will be 5 stitches on right needle), join a second doubled strand of yarn, bind off the center 14 stitches, knit to end.

Place last 7 (7, 8) stitches just worked on a stitch holder and cut yarn.

Rejoin yarn to neck edge of first group of shoulder stitches, and work 1 purl row.

Binding off at the armhole edge (beginning of knit rows only), bind off 2 stitches at the beginning of the next knit row, then 3 stitches at the beginning of the following knit row.

Return stitches from holder to needle and rejoin yarn to armhole edge, ready to work a purl row.

Binding off at the armhole edge (beginning of purl rows only), bind off 2 (2, 3) stitches at the beginning of the next purl row, then 2 stitches at the beginning of the following purl row, then 3 stitches at the beginning of the next purl row.

Make front piece same as back.

SLEEVES

Cast on 20 (20, 22) stitches with two strands of yarn held together.

Working in stockinette stitch, increase 1 stitch at each side every 12 (10, 10) rows 4 (5, 5) times—28 (30, 32) stitches.

Work even until piece measures 16$\frac{1}{2}$" (17", 17$\frac{1}{2}$") from beginning, ending with a purl row.

Shape sleeve cap as follows:

Bind off 2 stitches at the beginning of the next 2 rows, then decrease 1 stitch at each side on the next knit row, then decrease 1 stitch at each side every 4 rows 3 times—16 (18, 20) stitches.

Bind off 2 stitches at the beginning of the next 6 rows, then decrease 1 stitch at each side every knit row 0 (1, 2) times.

Bind off remaining 4 stitches.

Make a second sleeve same as the first.

Finishing:

Sew shoulder seams, matching shoulder shaping.

Sew side and sleeve seams.

Sew sleeves into armholes.

Weave in ends.

Comparable Yarns:

Any smooth, worsted weight cotton or blend.

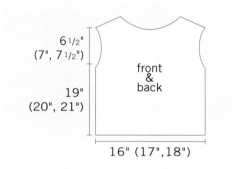

6$\frac{1}{2}$"
(7", 7$\frac{1}{2}$")

front
&
back

19"
(20", 21")

16" (17",18")

sleeve

22$\frac{1}{2}$"
(23$\frac{1}{2}$"
24$\frac{1}{2}$")

8$\frac{3}{4}$" (8$\frac{3}{4}$", 9$\frac{1}{2}$")

leather tie
cardigan

AREN'T YOU ALWAYS longing for the perfect cardigan—one that will go with almost all your clothes? Something you can throw over anything? This sweater is easy to wear with a very easy neckline and a versatile length—not too long and not too short. The leather tie makes it distinctive and helps avoid the prim look a lot of those buttoned-up sweaters tend toward. But I like to wear leather only as an accent because a bit goes a long way.

Knitting Level: Hot Knitters

Sizes: Small (medium, large)

Finished Measurements: 32" (34", 36") around

Materials:

5 (5, 5) skeins Suss Cotton (100% cotton; 174 yards; 113 grams/4 ounces), color #2 ivory

1 pair size 13 needles, or size to obtain gauge

2 pieces of leather, 1/2" wide and 12" long

Yarn needle

Gauge: 7 stitches = 3", or 2 1/3 stitches and 3 1/2 rows = 1", in stockinette stitch using double strand of yarn

How to Knit:

BACK

Cast on 38 (40, 42) stitches with two strands of yarn held together.

Work in stockinette stitch as follows:

Row 1: Knit all stitches.

Row 2: Purl all stitches.

Repeat these 2 rows for stockinette stitch until piece measures 12" (12 1/2", 13"), ending with a purl row.

Shape armhole as follows: Bind off 2 stitches at the beginning of the next 2 rows, then decrease 1 stitch at each side of the next knit row—32 (34, 36) stitches.

Work even (with no further shaping) until piece measures 19" (19 1/2", 20 1/2") from beginning, ending with a purl row.

Shape shoulders as follows: Bind off 2 stitches at the beginning of the next 4 rows, then bind off 2 (2, 3) stitches at the beginning of the next 2 rows.

LEFT: *Actress China Chow*
models my sexy cardigan.

Bind off remaining 20 (22, 22) stitches.

RIGHT FRONT

Cast on 19 (21, 23) stitches with two strands of yarn held together.

Work in stockinette stitch until piece measures 12" (12½", 13"), ending with a knit row.

Shape armhole and V neck at the same time as follows:

At the beginning of the next purl row, bind off 2 stitches once, then decrease 1 st at armhole edge (beginning of purl rows) once.

At the same time, decrease 1 stitch at neck edge (beginning of knit rows) every other row 10 (12, 13) times.

Work even on remaining 6 (6, 7) stitches until piece measures 19" (19½", 20½") from beginning, ending with a knit row.

Shape shoulder as follows: Bind off 2 stitches at armhole edge 2 times, then bind off 2 (2, 3) stitches at armhole edge once.

LEFT FRONT

Work same as right front, reversing all shaping. In other words, work armhole and shoulder shaping at beginning of knit rows, and V neck shaping at end of knit rows.

SLEEVES

Cast on 20 stitches with two strands of yarn held together.

Working in stockinette stitch, increase 1 stitch at each side every 8 rows 3 (4, 4) times—26 (28, 28) stitches.

Work even until piece measures 11" (12", 13") from beginning, ending with a purl row.

Shape sleeve cap as follows:

Bind off 2 stitches at the beginning of the next 2 rows, then decrease 1 stitch at each side on the next knit row, then decrease 1 stitch at each side every 4 rows 0 (1, 1) time—20 (20, 20) stitches.

Bind off 2 stitches at the beginning of the next 4 rows.

Bind off remaining 12 stitches.

Make a second sleeve same as the first.

Finishing:

Sew shoulder seams, matching bound-off rows.

Sew side and sleeve seams.

Sew sleeves into armholes.

Sew leather ties to front as shown.

Weave in ends.

Comparable Yarns:

Muench Samoa cotton-acrylic blend used double would give this cardigan a light touch.

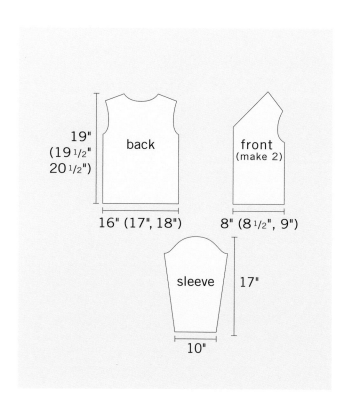

19" (19½", 20½")
back
16" (17", 18")

front (make 2)
8" (8½", 9")

sleeve   17"
10"

fitted ribbed
turtleneck

I MADE THIS OVERSIZED rust orange cowl neck turtle top for the famous *Scooby Doo* character Velma in the film version of the cartoon. Then I made forty-eight more fitted sweaters, some without sleeves, for the other characters in the movie. It's almost like a stretch sweater because the yarn is sort of chewy, weird, and spongy. Its long, fitted rib clings to your body.

LEFT: *This casual, comfortable sweater is lightweight but it has a heavy look thanks to its beautiful yarn.*

Knitting Level: Hot Knitters

Sizes: Small (medium, large)

Finished Measurements:

32" (34", 36") around

Materials:

12 (12, 13) skeins Muench Goa (50% cotton, 50% acrylic; 65 yards; 50 grams/1¾ ounces), color #06 orange

1 pair size 10 needles, or size to obtain gauge

1 16" circular needle size 10, or size to match other needles

3 stitch holders

Yarn needle

Gauge:

3¾ stitches and 4 rows = 1", in rib pattern, slightly stretched

How to Knit:

BACK

Cast on 48 (52, 56) stitches.

Work in knit 1, purl 1 rib as follows:

All Rows: *Knit 1, purl 1; repeat from * to end.

Repeat this row for 6 rows.

Beginning with the following row, increase 1 stitch at each side every 10 rows 7 times—62 (66, 70) stitches.

Work even (without further shaping) until piece measures 18½" from beginning.

Shape raglan armhole as follows: Bind off 4 stitches at the beginning of the next 2 rows, then decrease 1 stitch at each side every other row 16 (17, 18) times—22 (24, 26) stitches.

Work even if necessary until piece measures 22" (22½", 23") from beginning.

Place all stitches on a holder.

FRONT

Work same as back until piece measures 18½" from beginning.

Shape raglan armhole as for Back until 10 armhole decreases have been made—34 (38, 42) stitches.

Shape front neck as follows:

On the next decrease row, decrease 1 stitch, work until there are 7 (9, 11) stitches on right needle, bind off center 18 stitches, join second ball of yarn, work in pattern to last 2 stitches, decrease 1 stitch—7 (9, 11) stitches at each side.

Working each side separately, continue to decrease at armhole edges as established, and at the same time decrease 1 stitch at each neck edge every other row 2 (3, 4) times—no stitches remain.

SLEEVES

Cast on 34 (36, 38) stitches.

Working in knit 1, purl 1 rib, increase 1 stitch at each side every 10 rows 9 times—52 (54, 56) stitches.

Work even until piece measures 24" from beginning.

Shape raglan sleeve cap as follows:

Bind off 4 stitches at the beginning of the next 2 rows, then decrease 1 stitch at each side every other row 7 (8, 9) times, then decrease 1 stitch at each side every 3 rows 6 times - 18 stitches.

Bind off 6 stitches every other row twice.

Place remaining 6 stitches on a holder.

Make a second sleeve the same as the first.

Finishing:

Sew raglan seams, placing the edge of the sleeves with the stitch holder next to the back.

With 16" circular needle, beginning at the back, knit 22 (24, 26) stitches from back neck holder, knit 6 stitches from first sleeve holder, pick up and knit 7 stitches along upper edge of first sleeve, pick up and knit 24 (26, 28) stitches around front neck, pick up and knit 7 stitches along upper edge of second sleeve, knit 6 stitches from second sleeve holder—72 (76, 80) stitches.

Join and work knit 2, purl 2 rib in the round as follows:

All Rounds: *Knit 2, purl 2; repeat from * around.

Repeat this round until neck measures 10½", approximately 42 rows.

Bind off all stitches loosely.

Sew side and sleeve seams.

Weave in ends.

Comparable Yarns:

Any softly spun bulky cotton or cotton blend that matches the gauge and stretches easily.

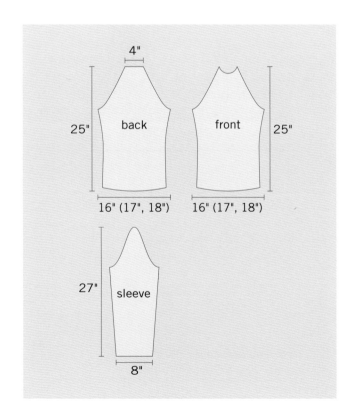

little girl
big heart pullover

ALTHOUGH THIS BASIC, boxy oversized sweater looks simple, it's actually one of the more challenging pieces in the book. The big heart is knit into the pattern, a technique called intarsia. The combination of the flat knit and fuzzy textured heart is unbeatable. Kids love to make everybody touch their heart!

The shape, my signature design, is unisex enough so that you could easily make this for a little boy in navy blue with a cream star. Or make it without the heart for an easy, basic pullover.

Knitting Level: Hot Knitters

Sizes: 1-2 (3-4, 5-6) years

Finished Measurements: 25" (26", 28") around

Materials:

3 (3, 3) skeins Suss Cotton (100% cotton; 174 yards; 113 grams/4 ounces), color #4 angel pink

1 skein Trendsetter Voila (100% nylon; 180 yards; 50 grams/1¾ ounces), color #10 hot pink

1 pair size 8 needles, or size to obtain gauge

1 16" circular needle size 7, or one size smaller than main needles

Yarn needle

Gauge:

4½ stitches and 5 rows = 1", in stockinette stitch using larger needles

How to Knit:

BACK

Cast on 55 (59, 63) stitches with Suss Cotton.

Work in stockinette stitch as follows:

Row 1: Knit all stitches.

Row 2: Purl all stitches.

Repeat these 2 rows for stockinette stitch until piece measures 14" (15", 17").

Bind off all stitches.

LEFT: *My little girl, Viveka, in her favorite Big Heart pullover. I named her after Swedish actress Viveka Lindfors.*

FRONT

Work as for back until piece measures 2" (3", 4"), ending with a purl row.

Establish heart pattern from chart as follows: Knit 10 (12, 14), work Row 1 of chart over center 35 stitches using doubled strand of Voila for heart, knit 10 (12, 14).

Maintaining stitches at each side in stockinette stitch with Suss Cotton, work until Row 39 of chart has been completed.

Cut Voila and continue in stockinette stitch in Suss Cotton only until piece measures 11" (12", 14") from beginning, ending with a purl row.

Shape neck as follows: Knit until there are 22 (23, 24) stitches on right needle, join second ball of yarn, bind off center 11 (13, 15) stitches, knit to end—22 (23, 24) stitches at each side.

Working each side separately, decrease 1 stitch at each neck edge every knit row 8 times—14 (15, 16) stitches at each side.

Work even (with no further shaping) until piece measures 14" (15", 17") from beginning.

Bind off all stitches.

SLEEVES

Cast on 28 (32, 32) stitches with Suss Cotton.

Working in stockinette stitch, increase 1 stitch at each side every 5 rows 11 times—50 (54, 54) stitches.

Work even until piece measures 11" (12", 13") from beginning.

Bind off all stitches.

Make a second sleeve same as the first.

Finishing:

Sew shoulder seams.

With 16" circular needle, pick up and knit 60 (62, 66) stitches evenly around neck opening.

Join and work stockinette stitch in the round (knit all stitches every round) until neck measures 3". Bind off all stitches loosely.

Sew sleeves to front and back, centering them on the shoulder seams.

Sew side and sleeve seams.

Weave in ends.

Comparable Yarns:

Jaeger Como (90% merino wool, 10% polyamide; 142 yards; 50 grams/1¾ ounces) is a good substitute because it is very light.

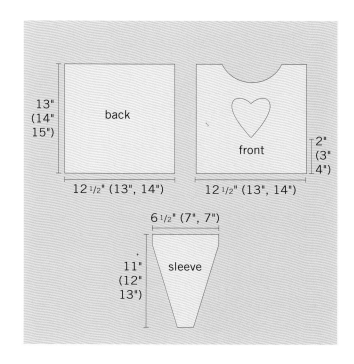

men's
dressy sweater

I FIRST MADE THIS for Keanu Reeves in *The Matrix II*. It's a dressy, very loose mesh knit that works well for evening all year round. The lightweight, mercerized, all-cotton, 2-ply yarn, with a special extrashiny finish, makes it great for summer. Guys love it because it gets looser and looser as you wear it. For a conservative guy I'd knit it in khaki or white. A funky guy would get red or black. Play around with it!

It's a little more time-consuming to make a big pullover than some of the other smaller projects in the book, but it's not really difficult.

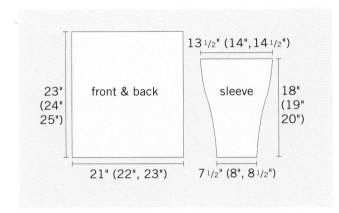

Knitting Level: Hot Knitters

Sizes: Small (medium, large)

Finished Measurements:

42" (44", 46") around

Materials:

4 (4, 4) skeins Suss Perle Cotton (100% cotton; 527 yards; 115 grams/4 ounces), color #101 pearl grey

1 pair size 10½ needles, or size to obtain gauge

2 stitch holders

Yarn needle

Gauge:

3½ stitches and 4½ rows = 1", in stockinette stitch using double strand of yarn

LEFT: *Swedish artist Ole Olofson wears a sweater I originally designed for Keanu Reeves in* The Matrix II.

How to Knit:

BACK

Cast on 74 (78, 82) stitches with two strands of yarn held together.

Work in stockinette stitch as follows:

Row 1: Knit all stitches.

Row 2: Purl all stitches.

Repeat these 2 rows for stockinette stitch until piece measures 23" (24", 25") from beginning.

Bind off 21 (22, 23) stitches.

Cut yarn and place center 32 (34, 36) stitches on a holder.

Rejoin yarn at neck edge and bind off remaining 21 (22, 23) stitches.

Make front same as back.

SLEEVES

Cast on 26 (28, 30) stitches with two strands of yarn held together.

Working in stockinette stitch, increase 1 stitch at each side every 7 rows 11 times—48 (50, 52) stitches.

Work even until piece measures 18" (19", 20") from beginning.

Bind off all stitches.

Make a second sleeve same as the first.

Finishing: Sew left shoulder seam.

Place stitches from back and front neck holders on one needle for neck—64 (68, 72) stitches.

Work back and forth in stockinette stitch until neck measures 2".

Bind off all stitches loosely.

Sew right shoulder and neck seam.

Sew sleeves to front and back, centering them on the shoulder seams.

Sew side and sleeve seams.

Weave in ends.

Comparable Yarns:

Brown Sheep Company Cotton Fleece works well, but if you substitute, do not use doubled yarn.

two tone
halter top

HOLLY HUNTER LOVES my halter tops and bought a few the last time she was in my store. For evening, I knit this little top in two colors, red and hot pink, but you could do it in black, too. Either way, you could wear it with a leather skirt or black slacks. The yarn is shiny with rough texture but still soft. It has a mock turtleneck and ties in the back. With an open back and open shoulders, the halter is quite sexy.

Knitting Level: Hot Knitters

Sizes: Small (medium, large)

Finished Measurements:

26" (28", 30") around

Materials: 2 skeins Muench Raffinesse (45% cotton, 35% polyester, 20% rayon; 104 yards; 50 grams/1$3/4$ ounces), color #6 pink

2 skeins Muench Raffinesse (45% cotton, 35% polyester, 20% rayon; 104 yards; 50 grams/1$3/4$ ounces), color #8 red

1 pair size 7 needles, or size to obtain gauge

Yarn needle

Gauge:

4$1/4$ stitches and 6$1/2$ rows = 1" in stockinette stitch

How to Knit:

BACK

Cast on 56 (60, 64) stitches with red.

Work in stockinette stitch as follows:

Row 1: Knit all stitches.

Row 2: Purl all stitches.

Repeat these 2 rows for stockinette stitch until piece measures 8", approximately 52 rows, ending with a purl row.

LEFT: *I've known Noelle Beck since my first days in New York when she starred in a daytime soap opera.*

Change to pink and work in stockinette stitch until piece measures 12" (12½", 13¼") from beginning, approximately 26 (30, 34) rows with pink.

Bind off all stitches.

FRONT

Work same as back, ending with a purl row, but do not bind off all stitches.

Shape upper front as follows: Bind off 3 stitches at the beginning of the next 2 rows, then decrease 1 stitch each side every knit row 12 (13, 14) times—26 (28, 30) stitches remaining.

Bind off all stitches.

NECKBAND

Cast on 108 stitches with pink.

Work in knit 1, purl 1 rib as follows for 6 rows:

All Rows: *Knit 1, purl 1; repeat from * to end.

Bind off all stitches.

Finishing:

Sew side seams.

Position center of neckband at center front neck and sew to front. Tie in back as shown.

Weave in ends.

Comparable Yarns:

Non-stretchy blends of nylon or microfiber.

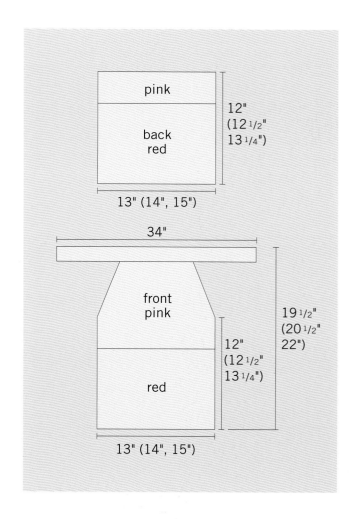

turtle
top

I FIRST MADE THIS sleeveless sweater for a magazine spread with Helen Hunt. It looked great on her, but it's flattering to anyone and very comfortable. The wool yarn is not at all itchy, and the neck is a little wide. This top goes perfectly with jeans, which is how Helen Hunt modeled it.

It looks harder to knit than it is. Basically you just start knitting and leave the bottom cropped, with no ribbing, which is what makes it look hip and unfinished.

Knitting Level: Hot Knitters

Sizes: Small (medium, large)

Finished Measurements:

30" (33½", 37") around

Materials:

5 (5, 6) skeins Muench Trikolore (100% wool; 77 yards; 100 grams/3½ ounces), color #28 multicolor

1 pair size 13 needles, or size to obtain gauge

Yarn needle

Gauge:

2½ stitches and 3½ rows = 1" in stockinette stitch

How to Knit:

BACK AND FRONT

Cast on 40 (44, 48) stitches.

Work in stockinette stitch as follows:

Row 1: Knit all stitches.

Row 2: Purl all stitches.

Repeat these 2 rows for stockinette stitch until piece measures 12" (13", 13½"), ending with a purl row.

Shape armhole as follows: Bind off 2 stitches at the beginning of the next 2 rows, then decrease 1 stitch at each side of the next 2 knit rows—32 (36, 40) stitches remain.

Work even (with no further shaping) until armhole measures

LEFT: *Actress and writer Julia Sweeney took my knitting class and knits for her adorable daughter all the time.*

6½ (6½, 7") above bound off stitches.

Shape shoulders as follows:

Bind off 2 (3, 3) stitches at the beginning of the next 4 rows, then bind off 3 (3, 3) stitches at the beginning of the next 2 rows—18 (18, 22) stitches remain.

Change to knit 1, purl 1 rib and work as follows for turtleneck:

All Rows: *Knit 1, purl 1; repeat from *to end.

Repeat this row until neck measures 9" from beginning of rib pattern.

Bind off all stitches loosely.

Make front piece same as back.

Finishing:

Sew shoulder seams.

Sew neck seams from shoulder to top, reversing the seam allowances halfway up so right side of seams will show when turtleneck is folded down.

Sew side seams.

Weave in ends.

Comparable Yarns:

Any bulky, single-ply wool.

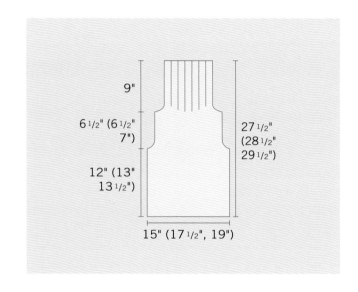

chunky striped
men's pullover

THIS IS A FOLDOVER TURTLENECK that is very comfortable—so important to men. It's loose knit in a heavy wool blend and boxier than the man's sweater on page 98, which is a finer knit. The uneven, asymmetrical stripes give it a nice casual look, good for knocking around in or going out to a movie. It can also look great in blues or greens.

Knitting Level: Hot Knitters

Sizes: Small (medium, large)

Finished Measurements: 43" (45", 47") around

Materials:

8 skeins Classic Elite Montera (50% llama, 50% wool; 127 yards; 100 grams/3½ ounces), color #3876 chocolate

8 skeins Classic Elite Montera (50% llama, 50% wool; 127 yards; 100 grams/3½ ounces), color #3848 blue

1 pair size 9 needles, or size to obtain gauge

1 16" circular needle size 8, or one size smaller than main needles

1 stitch holder

Yarn needle

Gauge:

3¾ stitches and 5 rows = 1", in stockinette stitch using double strand of yarn

How to Knit:

BACK

Cast on 80 (84, 88) stitches with chocolate.

Work in knit 2, purl 2 rib as follows:

All Rows: *Knit 2, purl 2; repeat from * to end.

Repeat this row for 12 rows.

Change to blue and work in stockinette stitch as follows:

Row 1: Knit all stitches.

Row 2: Purl all stitches.

Repeat these 2 rows for stockinette stitch in stripe pattern of 12 rows blue, 12 rows chocolate until piece measures 16½" (17", 18") from beginning, ending with a purl row.

Shape armhole as follows: Bind off 3 stitches at the beginning of the next 2 rows, then decrease 1 stitch at each side every knit row 6 (7, 8) times—62 (64, 66) stitches.

Work even (with no further shaping) until piece measures 26" (27", 28") from beginning, ending with a purl row.

Shape shoulders as follows: Bind off 3 stitches at the beginning of the next 10 rows.

Place remaining 32 (34, 36) stitches on a holder.

FRONT

Work same as back until piece measures 25" (26", 27") from beginning, ending with a purl row—62 (64, 66) stitches.

Shape neck as follows: Knit until there are 21 stitches on right needle, join second ball of yarn, bind off center 20 (22, 24) stitches, knit to end—21 stitches at each side.

Working each side separately, bind off 2 stitches at each neck edge every other row 3 times—15 stitches at each side.

Work even until piece measures 26" (27", 28") from beginning, ending with a purl row.

Shape shoulders as follows: Bind off 3 stitches at each armhole edge 5 times.

RIGHT SLEEVE

Cast on 36 (40, 40) stitches with chocolate.

Working in knit 2, purl 2 rib pattern for 12 rows.

Change to stockinette stitch and work with blue for 44 (48, 50) rows ending with a purl row, then work with chocolate to end of sleeve, and at the same time increase 1 stitch at each side every 5 rows 15 (14, 5) times, then increase 1 stitch at each side every 0 (6, 6) rows 0 (1, 10) times—66 (70, 70) stitches.

Work even until piece measures 18½" (19½", 20½") from beginning.

Shape sleeve cap as follows: Bind off 3 stitches at the beginning of the next 2 rows, then decrease 1 stitch at each side every knit row 5 times, then bind off 3 stitches at the beginning of the next 2 rows.

Bind off remaining 44 (48, 48) stitches.

LEFT SLEEVE

Cast on 36 (40, 40) stitches with chocolate.

Working in knit 2, purl 2 rib pattern for 12 rows.

Change to stockinette stitch and blue and shape as for right sleeve according to the following stripe pattern: 38 (42, 44) rows blue, 12 rows chocolate, 12 rows blue, 12 rows chocolate, work with blue to end.

Finishing:

Sew shoulder seams.

With 16" circular needle, knit 32 (34, 36) stitches from back neck holder, then pick up and knit 36 (38, 40) stitches around shaped front neck edge—68 (72, 76) stitches.

Join and work knit 2, purl 2 rib in the round as follows:

All Rounds: *Knit 2, purl 2; repeat from * around.

LEFT: *My husband, Brian, is my business manager as well as an actor.*

Repeat this round for 14 rounds, then increase 1 stitch at each shoulder seam every 4 rows 4 times, working new stitches into knit 2, purl 2 pattern—76 (80, 84) stitches.

Work even for 14 more rounds.

Bind off all stitches loosely.

Sew side and sleeve seams.

Sew sleeves into armholes.

Weave in ends.

Comparable Yarns:

Single-ply bulky wools or wool blends to retain softness.

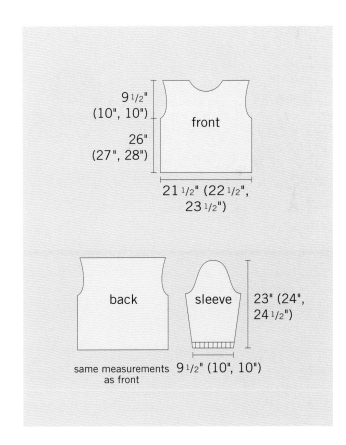

9½" (10", 10")

26" (27", 28")

front

21½" (22½", 23½")

back

same measurements as front

sleeve

9½" (10", 10")

23" (24", 24½")

single button
serendipitous cardigan

THIS IS THE SWEATER I made for Kate Beckinsale to wear in the movie *Serendipity*. In one scene she is skating in New York's Central Park and they wanted something she could move in, not too fitted and feminine. The sweater looked beautiful on her—it's not too long, and it hits the hip at just the right place. Although a fairly heavy wool, you can wear this piece all year round as a wrap to bring with you in case it gets chilly in the evening. I used a shell button instead of wood to make it a bit more elegant.

LEFT: *This great cardigan looks just perfect on my friend Julianne Moore.*

Knitting Level: Hot Knitters

Sizes: Small (medium, large)

Finished Measurements: 32" (34", 36") around

Materials:

6 (6, 7) skeins Muench Trikolore (100% wool; 77 yards; 100 grams/3$\frac{1}{2}$ ounces), color #32 multicolor

1 pair size 13 needles, or size to obtain gauge

1 shell or wood button, size 1"

Crochet hook size I

Yarn needle

Gauge:

2$\frac{1}{4}$ stitches and 3$\frac{1}{2}$ rows = 1", in stockinette stitch

How to Knit:

BACK

Cast on 36 (38, 40) stitches.

Work in stockinette stitch as follows:

Row 1: Knit all stitches.

Row 2: Purl all stitches.

Repeat these 2 rows for stockinette stitch until piece measures 14" (14$\frac{1}{2}$", 15"), ending with a purl row.

Shape armhole as follows: Bind off 2 stitches at the beginning of the next 2 rows, then decrease 1 stitch at each side of the next knit row—30 (32, 34) stitches.

Work even (with no further shaping) until piece measures 20" (21", 22") from beginning, ending with a purl row.

Shape shoulders as follows: Bind off 3 stitches at the beginning of the next 4 rows.

Bind off remaining 18 (20, 22) stitches.

LEFT FRONT

Cast on 19 (20, 21) stitches.

Work in stockinette stitch until piece measures 14" (14½", 15"), ending with a purl row.

Shape armhole as follows: Bind off 2 stitches at beginning of next row, then decrease 1 stitch at beginning of the following knit row—16 (17, 18) stitches.

Work even until piece measures 19" (20", 21") from beginning, ending with a knit row.

Shape neck and shoulder as follows:

Bind off 3 stitches at the beginning of the next purl row for neck edge, then decrease 1 stitch at neck edge (end of knit rows, beginning of purl rows) every row 7 (8, 9) times—6 (6, 6) stitches.

At the same time, when piece measures 20" (21", 22") from beginning, bind off 3 stitches at armhole edge 2 times.

RIGHT FRONT

Work same as left front, reversing armhole shaping by binding off at beginning of purl rows, until piece measures 18" (19", 20") from beginning, ending with a purl row—16 (17, 18) stitches.

Make buttonhole on the next knit row as follows: Knit 2, yarn over, knit 2 together, knit to end.

On the following row, work the yarn over as a purl stitch.

Work even until piece measures 19" (20", 21") from beginning, ending with a purl row.

Shape neck and shoulder as for left front, reversing shaping by binding off at beginning of knit rows for neck and beginning of purl rows for armhole.

SLEEVES

Cast on 18 (20, 20) stitches.

Working in stockinette stitch, increase 1 stitch at each side every 12 (10, 10) rows 4 (5, 5) times—26 (30, 30) stitches.

Work even until piece measures 19" (20", 21") from beginning, ending with a purl row.

Shape sleeve cap as follows: Bind off 2 stitches at the beginning of the next 2 rows, then decrease 1 stitch at each side every 4 rows 2 times, then every other row 4 times.

Bind off remaining 10 (14, 14) stitches.

Make a second sleeve same as the first.

Finishing:

Sew shoulder seams.

Sew side and sleeve seams.

Sew sleeves into armholes.

Work 1 row single crochet around front opening of cardigan.

Weave in ends.

Sew button to left front to correspond to buttonhole.

Comparable Yarns: Any bulky wool.

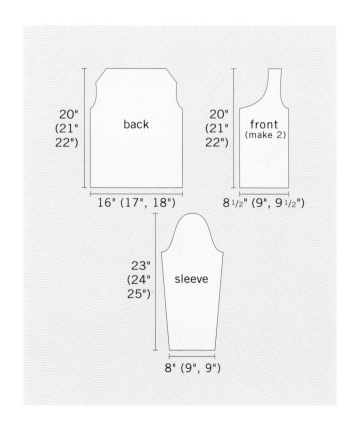

bell sleeved
cabled pullover

very winsome when she modeled this fitted cable pullover sweater with the big neck pulled way up over her chin on the cover of *InStyle Magazine.*

Knit it in navy, and wear with your khakis when you're hanging out during holidays in front of the fireplace—cozy. The ribbing is not too hard to knit and makes it very stylish and slimming. It's a heavy yarn, but you knit in big needles so it's fragile looking, almost like spider webs.

Knitting Level: Hot Knitters

Sizes: Small (medium, large)

Finished Measurements: 36" (38", 40") around

Materials:

8 (8, 9) skeins Classic Elite Yarns LaGran (76.5% mohair, 17.5% wool, 6% nylon; 90 yards; 42.5 grams/1½ ounces), color #6519 baby pink

1 pair size 13 needles, or size to obtain gauge

Cable needle

Yarn needle

LEFT: *Actress Maud Adams, who starred in three James Bond movies with Roger Moore, looks pretty in pink.*

Gauge:

2½ stitches and 4½ rows = 1", in stockinette stitch

How to Knit:

BACK

Cast on 46 (48, 50) stitches.

Work in stockinette stitch as follows:

Row 1: Knit all stitches.

Row 2: Purl all stitches.

Repeat these 2 rows for stockinette stitch for 20 rows, ending with a purl row.

Beginning with the next knit row, decrease 1 stitch at each side every 10 rows 3 times—40 (42, 44) stitches.

Work even (without further shaping) for 10 (12, 14) more rows, ending with a purl row.

Beginning with the next knit row, increase 1 stitch at each side every 6 rows 4 times—48 (50, 52) stitches.

Work even until piece measures 18½" (19½", 19") from beginning, ending with a purl row.

Shape armhole as follows: Bind off 3 stitches at the beginning of the next 2 rows, then decrease 1 stitch at each side every other row 3 times—36 (38, 40) stitches.

Work even until piece measures 23½" (24½", 24½") from beginning, ending with a purl row.

Shape shoulders as follows: Bind off 2 (3, 3) stitches at the beginning of the next 4 (6, 6) rows, then bind off 3 stitches at the beginning of the next 2 (0, 0) rows—22 (20, 22) stitches.

On the next knit row, decrease 1 (increase 1, decrease 1) stitch—21 stitches.

Purl 1 row.

Change to knit 3, purl 3 rib and work as follows:

Row 1: *Knit 3, purl 3; repeat from * to last 3 stitches, end knit 3.

Row 2: *Purl 3, knit 3; repeat from * to last 3 stitches, end purl 3.

Repeat these 2 rows for 10 rows, then increase 1 stitch at each side every 4 rows 7 times, working increased stitches into knit 3, purl 3 rib—35 stitches.

Work even (without further shaping) until rib section measures 10".

Bind off all stitches loosely.

FRONT

Cast on 48 (50, 52) stitches.

Work in stockinette stitch for 10 rows, ending with a purl row.

Establish center cable as follows: Knit 21 (22, 23), slip the next 3 stitches to cable needle and hold in back, knit 3, knit 3 from cable needle, knit to end.

Work 9 rows stockinette stitch, beginning and ending with a purl row.

Repeat the last 10 rows for cable pattern throughout, and at the same time, beginning with the next knit row, decrease 1 stitch at each side every 10 rows 3 times—42 (44, 46) stitches.

Work even for 10 (14, 12) more rows, ending with a purl row.

Beginning with the next knit row, increase 1 stitch at each side every 6 rows 4 times—50 (52, 54) stitches.

Work even until piece measures 18½" (19½", 19") from beginning, ending with a purl row.

Shape armhole as follows: Bind off 3 stitches at the beginning of the next 2 rows, then decrease 1 stitch at each side every other row 3 times—38 (40, 42) stitches.

Work even until piece measures 22" (23", 23") from beginning, ending with a purl row.

Shape front neck as follows: Knit until there are 10 (12, 12) stitches on right needle, join a new ball of yarn, bind off center 18 (16, 18) stitches, work to end—10 (12, 12) stitches at each side.

Working each side separately, decrease 1 stitch at each neck edge every knit row 3 times—7 (9, 9) stitches at each side.

Work even until piece measures 23½" (24½", 24½") from beginning, ending with a purl row.

Shape shoulders as follows: Bind off at each armhole edge 2 (3, 3) stitches 2 (3, 3) times, then bind off 3 stitches 1 (0, 0) time.

SLEEVES

Cast on 30 stitches.

Work in knit 3, purl 3 rib as follows:

All Rows: *Knit 3, purl 3; repeat from end.

Repeat this row for 30 rows, then change to stockinette stitch, and at the same time beginning with Row 21, shape bell sleeve by decreasing 1 stitch at each side every 20 (20, 24) rows 2 times—26 stitches.

Work even in stockinette stitch until piece measures 13½" (14½", 14½") from beginning, ending with a purl row.

Beginning with the next knit row, increase 1 stitch at each side every 4 rows 4 (4, 5) times—34 (34, 36) stitches.

Work even until piece measures 18" (19", 20") from beginning, ending with a purl row.

Shape sleeve cap as follows: Bind off 3 stitches at the beginning of the next 2 rows, then decrease 1 stitch at each side every 3 rows 6 times, then every other row 2 times—12 (12, 14) stitches.

Bind off all stitches.

Make a second sleeve the same as the first. Join left shoulder seam.

Finishing: With knit side of work facing you, join yarn to front at left shoulder and pick up and knit 21 stitches evenly along shaped front neck edge.

Purl 1 row.

Change to knit 3, purl 3 rib and work as follows:

Row 1: *Knit 3, purl 3; repeat from * to last 3 stitches, end knit 3.

Row 2: *Purl 3, knit 3; repeat from * to last 3 stitches, end purl 3.

Repeat these 2 rows for 10 rows, then increase 1 stitch at each side every 4 rows 7 times, working increased stitches into knit 3, purl 3 rib—35 stitches.

Work even until rib section measures 10".

Bind off all stitches loosely.

Sew second shoulder and neck seams, reversing the seam allowance halfway up the neck so right side will show when neck is folded down.

Sew side and sleeve seams.

Sew sleeves into armholes.

Weave in ends.

Comparable Yarns: Any mohair or mohair blend that matches the gauge.

10"

front
&
back

25"
(26"
26")

18" (19",20")

sleeve

23"
(24"
25")

12"

suss

resources

yarns used in suss designs

You can find all these yarns at Suss Design or at www.sussdesign.com, in addition to the suppliers listed on the next page.

Angel Hand-dyed Angora: Lorna's Laces, Yarns By Design

Aspen: Muench Yarns, Yarns By Design

Colinette: Diamond Yarn, Unique Kolours

Como Jaeger: Diamond Yarn

Eyelash: Trendsetter at Yarnsmith, Yarnxpress

Goa: Muench Yarns, Yarns By Design

LaGran: Classic Elite Yarns

Lame: Muench Yarns, Yarns By Design

Lamb's Pride: Brown Sheep Company, Yarnsmith

Lush: Classic Elite Yarns

Marokko: Muench Yarns, Yarns By Design

Montera: Classic Elite Yarns

Naturwolle: Muench Yarns, Yarns By Design

Raffinesse: Muench Yarns, Yarns By Design

Samoa: Muench Yarns, Yarns By Design

Touch Me: Muench Yarns, Yarns By Design

Trikolore: Muench Yarns, Yarns By Design

Voila: Trendsetter at Yarnsmith, Yarnxpress

yarn suppliers

See if your local yarn stores carry the yarns used in the book. Otherwise, you can try contacting the yarn companies here for a list of stores that carry their yarns.

AURORA YARNS
P.O. Box 3068
Moss Beach, CA 94038
(650) 728-2730

BAABAJOES WOOL COMPANY
P.O. Box 260604
Lakewood, CO 80226
www.baabajoeswool.com

BERROCO, INC.
14 Elmdale Road
P.O. Box 367
Uxbridge, MA 01569
(508) 278-2527
www.berroco.com

BROWN SHEEP COMPANY, INC.
100662 County Road 16
Scottsbluff, NE 69357
(308) 635-2198
www.brownsheep.com

CLASSIC ELITE YARNS, INC.
300 A Jackson Street
Lowell, MA 01852
(978) 453-2837
www.classiceliteyarns.com

COATS & CLARK
P.O. Box 12229
Greenville, SC 29612
(800) 648-1479
www.coatsandclark.com

DIAMOND YARN
9697 Street Laurent
Montreal PQ H3L 2N1
Canada
(514) 388-6188
www.diamondyarn.com

JCA
35 Scales Lane
Townsend, MA 01469
(978) 597-8794

LION BRAND YARN COMPANY
34 West 15th Street
New York, NY 10011
(800) 258-9276
www.lionbrand.com

MUENCH YARNS
285 Bel Marin Keys Boulevard
Novato, CA 94949
(415) 883-6375
www.muenchyarns.com

PLYMOUTH YARNS
P.O. Box 28
Bristol, PA 19007
(215) 788-0468
www.plymouthyarn.com

SAKONNET PURLS
3988 Main Road
Tiverton, RI 02878
(888) 624-9902
www.sakonnetpurls.com

SKACEL COLLECTION
P.O. Box 88110
Seattle, WA 98138
www.skacelknitting.com

TAHKI STACY CHARLES, INC.
8000 Cooper Avenue Building 1
Glendale, NY 11385
(800) 338-9276

UNIQUE KOLOURS
1428 Oak Lane
Downington, PA 19335
(800) 252-3934
www.uniquekolours.com

knitting websites

These websites offer everything from step-by-step knitting instruction to patterns to yarns and other knitting supplies.

THE KNITTER
www.theknitter.com

THE KNITTING GUILD OF AMERICA
www.tkga.com

THE KNITTING PAGES
www.knittingpages.com

THE WOOL CONNECTION
www.woolconnection.com

WOOLWORKS: THE ONLINE KNITTING COMPENDIUM
www.woolworks.org

YARNS BY DESIGN
www.yarnsbydesign.com

YARNSMITH
www.yarnsmith.com

YARNXPRESS
www.yarnxpress.com

suss shopping

Visit the Suss Design website to purchase knitting kits, my knitwear, and other goodies at www.sussdesign.com.

Suss Design for women is available at:

SUSS DESIGN
7350 Beverly Boulevard
Los Angeles, CA 90036

And at these stores found around the country:

ALABAMA

RUBY'S
2815 18th Street South
Homewood, AL 35209

CALIFORNIA

THE QUEEN BEE
1617 Westcliff Drive
Newport Beach, CA 92660

RABAT
2080 Chestnut Street
San Francisco, CA 94123

WINK & TWINKLE
12925 El Camino Real
San Diego, CA 92130

COLORADO

BOOGIES DINER
534 East Copper Avenue
Aspen, CO 81611

GARBARINI
3003 E. 3rd Ave
Denver, CO 80206

KISHMIR AT THE PEAKS
136 Country Club Drive
Telluride, CO 81435

DELAWARE

SOLE
110 Reheboth Avenue
Reheboth Beach, DE 19971

FLORIDA

CMJ ENTERPRISES
13100 SW 128 Street
Miami, FL 33186

EXIT ART
201 Gulf of Mexico Drive
Longboat Key, FL 34228

ILLINOIS

AMI AMI
720 Waukegan Road
Deerfield, IL 6015

ETRE
1361 Northwells
Chicago, IL 60610

MAINE

JOSEPH'S
410 Fore Street
Portland, ME 04101

MASSACHUSETTS

GILDAS
101 Union Street
Newton, MA 02459

MIDNIGHT FARM
18 Water Cromwell Lane
Vineyard Haven, MA 02568

VIA VAI
58 JFK Street
Cambridge, MA 02138

NEW JERSEY

BUTTERFLY KISSES
85 Brighton Avenue
West End, NJ 07740

NEW YORK

BARNEY'S
660 Madison Avenue
New York, NY 10021

BY NIGHT/ICE BLUE
1225 Madison Ave.
New York, NY 10128

HENRI BENDEL
12 West 57th Street
New York, NY 10019

SEARLE
119 West 40th Street
New York, NY 10018

NORTH CAROLINA

FRESH
813 Providence Road
Charlotte, NC 28207

PENNSYLVANIA

ANTHROPOLOGIE
1809 Walnut Street
Philadelphia, PA 19103
Also carried in the
Anthropologie catalog

TEXAS

WINK
2429 Bissonnet
Houston, TX 77005

WYOMING

TETON CLOTHING AND
HOME COLLECTIONS
105 E. Broadway
Jackson, WY 83001

*Suss Design for children is available
through the Garnet Hill Catalog as well
as the following stores:*

ALABAMA

RUBY'S
2815 18th Street South
Homewood, AL 35209

CALIFORNIA

BABY WRIGHTS
1146 Highland Avenue
Manhattan Beach, CA 9026

THE RED BALLOON
280 N. Main Street
Santa Ana, CA 92705

COLORADO

KISS THE MOON
234 Gore Creek Drive
Vail, CO 81658

IDAHO

BRASS RANCH RIVER RUN
520 River Run Plaza
Ketchum, ID 83340

ILLINOIS

MADISON AND FRIENDS
940 N. Rush Street
Chicago, IL 60611

MASSACHUSETTS

PINWHEELS
7 South Beach
Nantucket, MA 02554

NEW JERSEY

EAT YOUR SPINACH
11 S. Broad Street
Ridgewood, NJ 07450

MARCIA'S ATTIC
213 Main Street
Fort Lee, NJ 07024

NEW YORK

BARNEY'S
660 Madison Avenue
New York, NY 10021

TAKASHIMAYA
693 Fifth Avenue
New York, NY 10022

Z BABY COMPANY
210 E. 95th Street
New York, NY 10128

SOUTH CAROLINA

ISLAND CHILD
The Village at Wexford
Hilton Head Island, SC 29938

TEXAS

GOODNIGHT MOON
108 Preston Royal Shopping Center
Dallas, TX 75223

LITTLE PATOOTIES
2608 Westheimer
Houston, TX 77098

glossary of knitting terms

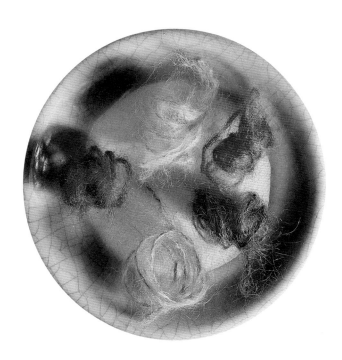

Decrease: One way is to reduce the number of stitches in a row by knitting 2 together.

Double pointed knitting needles: Needles with a point on either end. They can substitute for circular needles when knitting in the round is called for.

Dropped stitch: A stitch that falls off the needle, usually accidentally.

Garter stitch: The pattern that results when you knit every row.

Gauge: The number of stitches and rows per inch in a pattern.

Increase: One way is to add to the number of stitches in a row by knitting in front and back of a stitch.

Bind off: Finish off an edge and keep stitches from unraveling by knitting two stitches and lifting the first stitch over the second, the second over the third, etc. (In the U.K. this is called cast off.)

Cast on: Form a foundation row by making any number of loops on the knitting needle.

Circular knitting needles: Two short needles connected by a nylon or plastic cord.

Knit: The basic stitch in knitting made by inserting the needle from front to back.

Knitwise: Insert the needle into the stitch as if you were going to knit it.

Make one: With tip of the needle, lift strand between last stitch knitted and next stitch on left-hand needle, place strand on left-hand needle and knit into back of it to increase 1 stitch.

Place markers: Loop a piece of contrast yarn or purchased stitch marker onto the needle.

Pick up and knit: Knit into the loops along an edge.

Purl: A stitch made by inserting the needle from back to front; the opposite of the basic knitting stitch.

Purlwise: Insert the needle into the stitch as if you were going to purl it.

Reverse stockinette stitch: The pattern that results when you purl all right-side rows and knit all wrong-side rows.

Row: The width of a piece of knitting, based on the number of stitches first cast on to the needles.

Selvage stitch: Edge stitch that helps make seaming easier.

Skip: Skip specified number of crochet stitches of the previous row and work into next stitch. (In the U.K. this is called miss.)

Slip, slip, knit: Slip next 2 stitches knitwise, one at a time, to right-hand needle. Insert tip of left-hand needle into fronts of these stitches from left to right and knit them together to decrease 1 stitch.

Slip stitch: Pass a stitch from the left-hand to the right-hand needle as if to purl without working it.

Stockinette stitch: The pattern that results when you knit all right-side rows and purl all wrong-side rows.

Work even: Continue in specified pattern without increasing or decreasing. (In the U.K. this is called work straight.)

Yardage: A unit of measure for yarn, as opposed to its weight.

Yarn over: Make a new stitch by placing the yarn over the right-hand needle.

acknowledgments

I WOULD LIKE TO BELIEVE that my entire life is one big "thank you" to all of those people who brought me to this place today. I celebrate their generosity in what I do, and my giving back perpetuates this world of thankfulness that surrounds me.

Specifically, I thank my mother and grandmother for imparting their knitting legacy to me. Thanks also to all of you who, by taking part in my knitting nights over the years, have helped me sustain my craft. To all of the stores across the country that carry my designs and all of my loyal customers on Beverly Boulevard, thank you for helping knitting to flourish.

I am so lucky to have a business with such creative and hard working people surrounding me at Suss Design. I want to thank all of my employees for their artistry and commitment to my dream. Thanks to: Anna Karin Nordlund, who has become such a dear friend, for keeping me focused throughout the years; Kiki Toti and Kelly Canterbury Dimeo for their tireless creativity and hard work; Melissa Nelson, an extraordinary knitter and teacher, for pouring all of her expertise into this book; Al and Lorraine Natkin for initially investing in me with capital and continuing to invest love, enthusiasm, and great insight.

This book began in November 2000, when *People Magazine* published a feature on me and my knitwear for the movie *How the Grinch Stole Christmas.* I am thankful for Allison Gee who wrote the article; Kelly Cutrone and People's Revolution, who brought me to *People's* attention (and who continue to support me with great love and wisdom and vigilance); Rita Ryack, the brilliant Grinch costume designer, who let me share and play in her vision; Robin Dellabough of Lark Productions, who read the article, proposed this book idea in the first place, and who has been a wonderful partner in this throughout; Shiva Gold, my sister-in-law, who started writing with me on a whim, not knowing a real book deal was on the horizon; and to Constance Herndon and the team at Stewart, Tabori & Chang, who believed in this project and trusted Robin and me to see it through.

The pleasure is in the doing. Thank you Karen Knauer for photography that is so beautiful and rich and thrilling to the eye. Karen's visual sensibilities really define this book. Thanks to Robin Glaser, Lonnie Partridge, Malin Miramontes, and Susan Balcunas for contributions in styling and make-up.

Thanks to all of our wonderful models. Your willingness to be photographed made the book not only possible, but nearly perfect.

Julianne Moore – For your beautiful support over the years.
Kirsty Hume – You are wonderful and so down-to-earth.
Youki Kudoh – For wearing everything I make and looking great doing so.

Steven and Juliet Weber – For your love and enthusiasm and great sense of fun.

Alexis Oliphant – For letting me use your adorable baby.

Maud Adams – For being so lovely. You are my hero!

Noelle Beck – My very special friend. You have been with me since the beginning.

Regina King – So lovely and so amazing.

Anna Karin Nordlund – Always there in a pinch.

China Chow – For giving up your time. I love having you in the class.

Julia Sweeney – For your lust for life. You are incredible.

Ole Olofson – For being the guy who knits in a knitting book. I love your picture.

Nina Baik – For our chats together. You've become a great friend.

Nancy Baik – For making that turtleneck look even better.

Maria Springer – For wanting to participate. You are in good company.

Hanna Cousins – My older daughter. You have so much soul in you.

Viveka Cousins – My younger daughter. You are like a ray of sun.

Brian Cousins – The man who gets the best of me and my knitting.

Finally, I must give thanks to my friends and family, here, there, and gone. I have been so blessed with people who have always encouraged me and believed in me. I believe that my path has been filled with many angels and I am grateful to you all: Peter, Malin, Christer, and Tony, my siblings; Carin and Sven, my parents; Morfar Gunnar, Mormor Carla, Ingid, Anne, and Tommy, my relatives; Andrew Silverman, my American brother; Michael T. Smith and Maria Morreale; Seth Price and Eric Petterson; Eric and Penny Saftler; Richie and Leslie Abrams; Susan Balcunas; Laurie and Michael Della Femina; the Twills; Marcy(!).

index

Published in 2002 by
Stewart, Tabori & Chang
A Company of La Martinière Groupe
115 West 18th Street
New York, NY 10011

Export sales to all countries except Canada, France,
and French-speaking Switzerland:
Thames & Hudson, Ltd.
181A High Holborn
London WC1V 7QX
England

Canadian Distribution:
Canadian Manda Group
One Atlantic Avenue, Suite 105
Toronto, Ontario M6K 3E7
Canada

Library of Congress Cataloging-in-Publication Data

Cousins, Suss.
    Hollywood knits! : 30 original designs/by Suss Cousins;
        photography by Karen Knauer.
            p. cm.
    ISBN 1-58479-226-4
    1. Knitting—Patterns. I. Title

TT820 .C853 2002
746.43'2041—dc21

2002066829

The main text of this book was composed in Trade Gothic.
Printed in Singapore
10 9 8 7 6 5 4 3 2